OCCUPATIONS OF THE PEOPLE OF GREAT BRITAIN, 1801–1981

Occupations of the People of Great Britain, 1801–1981

Guy Routh

with a Compendium of a Paper 'Occupations of the People of the United Kingdom, 1801–81' by Charles Booth

First published 1987

Published by
THE MACMILLAN PRESS LTD
Houndmills, Basingstoke, Hampshire RG21 2XS
and London
Companies and representatives
throughout the world

Printed in Hong Kong

British Library Cataloguing in Publication Data
Routh, Guy
Occupations of the people of Great
Britain, 1801–1981.
1. Great Britain — Occupations — History
I. Title II. Booth, Charles. Occupations
of the people of the United Kingdom, 1801–81
331.7 '00941   HD8389
ISBN 0–333–43497–8

Contents

List of Tables and Figures

Tables

Figures

Preface

Charles Booth (1840–1916) was celebrated in his day and is remembered in ours for his *Life and Labour of the People in London*. It was in that great enterprise that Beatrice Webb, his cousin by marriage, served her apprenticeship. She afterwards remarked, 'the grand inquest into the conditions of life and labour of the four million inhabitants of the richest city in the world – an investigation carried on by Charles Booth (entirely at his own expense) over a period of seventeen years and published in as many volumes – seems to me to stand out as a landmark alike in social politics and in economic science' (Beatrice Webb, 1926, p. 226).

On 18 May 1886 Booth presented a paper to the Statistical Society (it had not yet been granted its Royal Charter) under the title of 'Occupations of the People of the United Kingdom, 1801–81'. The centenary of its presentation seems a good time to extend the survey to 1981. For the period 1911–71, I draw on a book published some years ago (Routh, 1980) which I now extend to incorporate the results of the census of 1981. For the intervening years, I pick up the story where Booth left it and carry it on to the point where I began.

Booth's paper of 1886, which is reproduced as Chapter 1 of this book, demonstrates how much can be deduced, and rightly deduced, from the careful assembly and consideration of census data:

> We know that Manufacture was then [in 1801] an adjunct of Agriculture, and that a hundred things were made at home for which everyone now goes to a shop; we know that machinery and commerce have changed this, and we see the end of the period of revolution in the amazing figures of change between 1841 and 1851, when the furthest point of unrestricted competition was reached, and when the reaction towards socialism commenced with the Factory Acts; but it is only of the period since 1851 that the census figures enable us to speak with any accuracy (see Chapter 1 below, p. 12).

Nowadays, of course, we have an abundance (some might say a superabundance) of figures. It is difficult to keep up with them, and still more so to interpret them correctly, tasks that I hope this book will do something to facilitate.

GUY ROUTH

Introduction

A worker's job consists of a set of duties that he or she is required to perform. Nowadays, they may be formalised in a written job description, but more generally they are defined by custom and practice. Jobs with similar characteristics are grouped into occupations. In an industry many jobs are assembled in that variety of occupations necessary to process the materials and produce the products by which it is characterised. Whether we take the viewpoint of job, occupation or industry, the process we observe is one of work which, in Booth's words, consists of 'the turning of raw materials into things serviceable' (see Chapter 1 below, p. 13), or, in the words of Eugen Loebl, 'the transformation of natural forces into useful forces, natural goods into useful goods'. 'The source of wealth thus lies in the degree to which we are able to transform and control natural forces, and this, in turn, is a direct result and a function of our ability to think and to create' (Loebl, 1976, p. 22).

In pre-capitalist societies innovation was regarded with suspicion. It still is in subsistence economies of the present day. When people live from hand to mouth, it is safer to rely on methods proved by practice and preserved by tradition. There is no end of cases where the bright ideas of townspeople, backed by government authority, have resulted in disaster. But the riches of the mercantile revolution brought with them scope for experiment. The variety of occupations expanded both with the invention of new products and the division of labour for the production of traditional ones. At the turn of the seventeenth century, Boisguillebert remarked on the growth of opulence: 'in the infancy or innocence of the world man's simple needs were procured by the pursuit of only three or four occupations; now there are more than two hundred, with more invented every day' (Boisguillebert, 1843, pp. 403–4). In 1861, the census authorities in London prepared a dictionary of occupations; by 1911, it contained 'upwards of 30,000 different terms' (*Census of England and Wales 1911*, vol. X, p. ix, Cd 7018, 1914).

The advent of the industrial system did not make work easier for the majority of workers. In agriculture they were required to work very hard at certain times of the year, in particular for planting and harvesting, but these were interspersed by periods when there was not much to do, and this lent variety to their lives. As the Industrial

Revolution proceeded, farm labour was replaced by work in factories and mines, where girls and boys, men and women were required to work for twelve or fourteen hours a day, six days a week.

Adam Smith, who in Book I of *The Wealth of Nations* had hailed the division of labour as the prime instrument of progress, in Book V warned of its evil implications:

> In the progress of the division of labour, the employment of the far greater part of those who live by labour, that is, of the great body of the people, comes to be confined to a few very simple operations; frequently to one or two. But the understandings of the greater part of men are necessarily formed by their ordinary employments. The man whose whole life is spent in performing a few simple operations, of which the effects too are, perhaps, always the same, has no occasion to exert his understanding, or to exercise his invention in finding out expedients for removing difficulties which never occur. He naturally loses, therefore, the habit of such exertion, and generally becomes as stupid and ignorant as it is possible for a human creature to become. The torpor of his mind renders him, not only incapable of relishing or bearing a part in any rational conversation, but of conceiving any generous, noble, or tender sentiment, and consequently of forming any just judgment concerning many even of the ordinary duties of private life... His dexterity at his own particular trade seems, in this manner, to be acquired at the expence of his intellectual, social, and martial virtues. But in every improved and civilized society this is the state into which the labouring poor, that is, the great body of people, must necessarily fall, unless government takes some pains to prevent it.
>
> (Adam Smith, 1776, pp. 781–2)

This was the state into which the labouring poor did indeed fall. Almost another century had to pass before compulsory education was introduced in England, while long struggles were waged to reduce hours and improve conditions of work, to raise wages and, eventually, to introduce pensions and sick and unemployment insurance. But all this time, a silent evolution was occurring that, when foreshortened by historical narration, assumes the appearance of a revolution. The labouring poor, for the first part of the nineteenth century, were held in a trap that left them little or no initiative and no means of escape. Sons and daughters followed fathers and mothers into coal-mines, textile factories or domestic service, with poverty now substituted for the feudal obligations of previous days. But erratically and slowly the boundaries of choice did expand.

The railways brought new jobs as well as possibilities of travel, the engineering industry offered new opportunities for the learning and exercise of skills. Restrictions on women's employment were eased by the expansion of nursing and teaching and, in the closing decades of the century, their entry into office work, aided by the invention of the typewriter. In the twentieth century there came substantial increases in the numbers of scientists and engineers, medical auxiliaries, draughtsmen and technicians. This book offers a measure of the extent of the transformation and the pace at which it has advanced, the data having been drawn mainly from the occupational tables of the censuses of population.

These censuses have been held every ten years, in the first year of each decade, beginning in 1801 and excepting 1941. As is to be expected, they have varied in quality and scope. In 1801, three occupational classes were distinguished: (1) agriculture, (2) trade, manufactures and handicrafts, and (3) the rest, with enumerators also required to report the numbers of army and navy personnel, merchant seamen, and convicts awaiting transportation. In 1811, the authorities decided that families were more important than individual workers: how many families were there whose existence depended on income derived from agriculture or trade, manufactures and handicrafts, or something else?

In 1841 there was an important organisational change: the task of enumeration was transferred from parish overseers, clergymen or schoolmasters to the recently established Registrars of Births and Deaths. Each householder was now required to complete a schedule under the supervision of enumerators appointed by the Registrars. 'These schedules were copied into books which were transmitted to the Census Office, where the work of classifying the occupations from the information supplied by the people themselves was carried out under definite rules and on uniform lines for the whole country' (*Census of England and Wales 1911*, vol. X, p. vi). The authorities were overwhelmed. In cotton manufacture alone 1255 different titles were returned. With attempts at classification abandoned, these were listed under the heading, 'Cotton manufacture, all branches'. Even so, the report ended up with 877 occupational headings, presented in alphabetical order with no attempt at further analysis.

In 1851, order was introduced by the allocation of occupations to

17 classes and 91 sub-classes. The dictionary of occupational terms in 1861 showed their allocation to 'Orders' and 'Sub-orders' (*ibid.*, p. vi). The agonising continued over the principles by which classification should be applied. A report to the Registrar General proposed that the criterion should be the substance on which the work was performed, so that persons working and dealing in animal substances were differentiated from those working and dealing in vegetable substances, mineral substances and so on (Appendix by W. Farr to the *Census Report, 1861*, p. 232).

It was not until 1911 that a solution emerged: there had to be two sets of tables, one classifying the occupied population by occupation (the sort of work performed), the other by industry (the end product by the relevant establishment). In 1921, this separation was more precisely established, and has since formed the basis of those census tables dealing with economic activity.

In 1911, there was another important innovation: every occupation was allocated to one of five social classes, a system that you will find elaborated in section 3.1 below. This was related to the Registrar General's analysis of occupational mortality (begun in 1851) and fertility (1911). Children per family do indeed vary significantly with social class, as does the expectation of life.

The classification system of 1921 marked a great step forward, but the difficulties of those working with census data were not over. The high-point of the census-taker's art was reached in 1951. In 1961, 1966 (an experimental sub-census) and 1971, the number of occupations distinguished was drastically reduced, while in 1961 the distinction between employer and manager was dropped (as it had been in the report of 1931). The distinction was reasserted in 1966, and, in 1981, the number of occupations was increased to 549 (still below the 584 units of 1951). In future, we may at least hope for consistency, if not perfection, for the Office of Census is committed to the Department of Employment's *Classification of Occupations and Directory of Occupational Titles* (CODOT), changes to which require the agreement of a number of departments. The system is explained in the Office of Population Censuses and Surveys, *Classification of Occupations and Coding Index* (HMSO, 1980).

G.R.

1 Charles Booth: 'Occupations of the People of the United Kingdom, 1801–81'*

1.1 GENERAL REVIEW OF OCCUPATION CENSUSES

Although it was not until 1831 that any detailed return of the occupations of the people was attempted, there had been in the earliest censuses a rough and ready method adopted of dividing the population into three or four large groups, with a view of distinguishing those who obtained their support directly from the land from those engaged in manufacture, trade or the learned professions. Thus in 1801 we find returns under three headings: (1) persons chiefly employed in agriculture; (2) persons chiefly employed in trade, manufacture, or handicraft; and (3) all other persons not employed in the two preceding classes. This return, it will be noted, is of individuals, but in 1811 and 1821 the number of *families* is substituted for individuals. The occupations are given in the same form, but it is the number of families chiefly employed in agriculture, or otherwise, that are stated. The principle on which the returns are based is, however, the same, and it is one on which I should wish to lay stress, viz., to ascertain the total number *supported* by each of the great branches of industry.

Resuming our review from 1821, we find in the next census (1831) the first attempt is made at any detailed enumeration of occupations; it is, however, of a very limited extent, being strictly confined to males aged 20 years and upwards, engaged in what are called 'retail trades and handicrafts'. The great bulk of the population are still summed up under a few headings as in the previous decades, though particulars are given under these headings of males over 20, and columns added for professional men and domestic servants.

The census of 1841 shows considerable advance in the details given. For the first time, all the principal occupations in the country are recorded, and the whole population is brought directly into the

*From a paper delivered in London to the Statistical Society on 18 May 1886.

1

tables of enumeration. There are separate returns for every county and for the large towns; the sexes are distinguished, but the ages are only given at two periods, under or over 20 years of age. Important, however, as was the advance made, it was exceeded in 1851, when the model on which the returns are still drawn up was originated. The great feature of this census is the grouping of occupations into seventeen classes with numerous sub-classes, the ages being given in quinquennial periods. The system of classification is as follows:

Class 1   Persons engaged in the Imperial or Local Government.

Class 2   Persons engaged in the defence of the country.

Class 3   Persons engaged in religion, law, or medicine.

Class 4   Persons engaged in art, literature, science and education.

Class 5   Persons engaged in household duties, as wives, children, etc.

Class 6   Persons engaged in boarding, lodging, domestic service and dress.

Class 7   Persons engaged in commercial pursuits (merchants, bankers, etc.)

Class 8   Persons engaged in conveyance.

Class 9   Persons engaged in agriculture.

Class 10   Persons engaged in breeding, animal tending and fishing.

Class 11   This class has been, with advantage, largely reduced. It was in 1851 supposed to include all those engaged in the higher branches of mechanical or chemical arts, and embraces artisans and mechanics, book-sellers and printers, the building trades, machine, tool and instrument makers, coach and shipbuilders, chemical manufacturers, dyers etc., and even persons engaged in the public amusement.

Class 12   Workers or dealers in animal substances, including family butchers and poulterers and all the woollen and silk operatives.

Class 13   Workers and dealers in vegetable substances, from the brewer to the upholsterer, from the paper manufacturer or cotton spinner to the greengrocer.

Class 14   Workers in mineral substances.

Class 15   Unskilled or unspecified labour.

Class 16   Persons of rank, property or independent means.

Class 17   Useless or disabled members of society, criminals, paupers, pensioners and others supported by the community; but the returns are very incomplete and misleading, for only those who failed to return themselves to a definite occupation are here included. The great majority of these classes having returned themselves as following, or having at some period of their lives followed, an occupation, have been returned with the regularly employed.

In the census for 1851 (which like its predecessors is for Great Britain) the separate tables for England and Wales, and for Scotland, contain the occupations summarised and brought within reasonable limits, the smaller divisions of labour being included under some broad or general heading to which they belong, or classed as 'others', but there are also tables for Great Britain which give details of all these minor forms of employment. In 1861 the returns for England and Scotland are no longer given in conjunction, but are placed in separate volumes, and the detailed table with further amplification is given for each country. The consequence is that the tables are rendered very bulky and unwieldy, and this becomes more striking on referring to the returns in the corresponding volume for 1871. Here the pruning knife has been very busy: the tables are reduced to a third of their former size, numbers of small trades are spirited away, and in their place appears a rather formidable item in the word others, for an explanation of which it is necessary to refer to the voluminous report.

Meanwhile, though the broad plan of classification remains much the same as in 1851, huge transpositions of numbers have been made from one class to another; the domestic class in one census includes the larger part of the population, and in the next is reduced by more than half; 350 000 persons in England alone (consisting of the wives and other relatives of farmers, etc.) are taken from the agricultural class of one census and placed in the unoccupied of another; the partially occupied wives are in no two successive censuses classed alike – and generally there is such a want of fixity of principle or method, that even competent authorities have been seriously misled regarding the apparent results. Possibly these changes were to a large extent necessary or unavoidable, but surely attention might have been drawn to them and some explanation given, instead of which there is not even so much as a footnote. The seeker after information is left to grope his way in the dark; if by chance he stumbles on the truth, well and good, if not he but adds his quota to the enormous total of false information before the public.

It was with the idea of remedying to some extent this state of things that I undertook the compilation of the tables, the results of which are submitted in [Table 1.1]. They do not contain any new or original information, but restate that given in the census in a more uniform and accessible shape.

Table 1.1   Occupations of the people of Great Britain, 1841–81 (in thousands and decimals of a thousand)

		1841	*1851*	*1861*	*1871*	*1881*
A. *Agriculture*						
Farmers and their	M	287.2	423.8	410.3	389.6	365.7
relatives	F	22.9	27.8	29.2	31.2	27.7
	All	310.1	451.6	439.5	420.8	393.4
Labourers and	M	1073.2	1257.1	1234.7	1042.3	932.6
Shepherds	F	81.1	198.2	131.5	101.7	84.5
	A	1154.3	1455.3	1366.2	1144.0	1017.1
Nurserymen,	M	58.8	95.3	101.0	121.2	87.1
Gardeners, etc.	F	1.6	2.8	2.3	3.0	3.5
	A	60.4	98.1	103.3	124.2	90.6
Drainage &	M	—	—	4.0	3.9	6.5
Machinery	F	—	—	—	—	0.1
Attendants	A	—	—	4.0	3.9	6.6
Breeding & Dealing	M	33.6	52.0	63.4	68.8	66.8
(Horses & Cattle)	F	0.1	1.2	0.2	0.4	0.5
	A	33.7	53.2	63.6	69.2	67.3
B. *Fishing*						
Fishermen	M	23.4	36.5	39.1	47.1	58.1
	F	0.4	—	1.4	1.4	2.9
	A	23.8	36.5	40.5	48.5	61.0
C. *Mining*						
Miners	M	188.4	298.1	379.6	432.8	506.6
	F	6.1	6.5	5.3	6.1	6.2
	A	194.5	304.6	384.9	438.9	512.8
Quarrying &	M	39.5	76.5	94.8	103.5	121.6
Brickmaking	F	0.6	2.1	2.6	3.4	3.3
	A	40.1	78.6	97.4	106.9	124.9
Salt & water works	M	1.7	3.6	4.3	5.4	7.2
	F	—	0.2	0.1	—	0.2
	A	1.7	3.8	4.4	5.4	7.4
D. *Building*						
Management	M	16.9	22.8	35.9	47.9	61.1
	F	0.1	0.8	0.1	—	0.1
	A	17.0	23.6	36.0	47.9	61.2
Operatives	M	361.7	455.2	524.4	641.5	759.0
	F	1.3	0.2	0.9	1.0	2.3
	A	363.0	455.4	525.3	642.5	761.3

		1841	1851	1861	1871	1881
Roadmaking	M	32.4	51.1	58.9	68.3	84.5
	F	—	—	—	—	0.3
	A	32.4	51.1	58.9	68.3	84.8
E. *Manufacture*						
Machinery & tools	M	59.4	108.1	168.7	211.7	247.9
	F	3.2	4.3	7.9	7.9	10.9
	A	62.6	112.4	176.6	219.6	258.8
Shipbuilding	M	25.9	31.3	53.1	61.5	72.6
	F	—	—	0.1	0.1	0.1
	A	25.9	31.3	53.2	61.6	72.7
Metal workers	M	204.8	307.3	393.2	468.1	517.7
	F	8.6	24.5	28.6	27.5	30.9
	A	213.4	331.8	421.8	495.6	548.6
Earthenware, etc.	M	25.1	37.4	45.7	53.8	55.8
	F	7.6	12.1	14.0	18.9	21.1
	A	32.7	49.5	59.7	72.7	76.9
Fuel, gas & chemicals	M	6.5	19.6	28.2	40.4	49.4
	F	0.4	1.9	1.9	4.5	4.6
	A	6.9	21.5	30.1	44.9	54.0
Furs, leather, glue,	M	35.0	48.9	51.8	54.5	54.6
etc.	F	2.6	6.8	9.0	10.9	14.1
	A	37.6	55.7	60.8	65.4	68.7
Wood, furniture &	M	166.7	202.7	226.0	238.4	248.5
carriages	F	4.9	9.2	15.4	21.5	20.8
	A	171.6	211.9	241.4	259.9	269.3
Paper, floorcloth &	M	9.9	15.4	17.1	24.4	29.7
waterproof	F	4.1	11.1	14.3	17.9	29.9
	A	14.0	26.5	31.4	42.3	59.6
Textiles & dyeing	M	450.8	575.2	523.8	489.3	457.6
	F	334.0	606.7	657.7	691.8	695.6
	A	784.8	1181.9	1181.5	1181.1	1153.2
Dress	M	390.2	452.7	425.7	409.7	391.2
	F	206.5	526.1	606.4	608.8	671.2
	A	596.7	978.8	1032.1	1018.5	1062.4
Food, drink &	M	96.5	139.2	154.3	168.1	179.2
smoking	F	8.5	13.5	17.2	20.9	33.2
	A	105.0	152.7	171.5	189.0	212.4
Watches, instruments	M	21.2	25.4	35.4	38.8	45.3
& toys	F	0.8	1.3	3.0	3.1	3.6
	A	22.0	26.7	38.4	41.9	48.9
Printing & bookbinding	M	24.8	35.0	48.0	65.7	84.9
	F	2.1	4.5	7.7	10.6	16.8
	A	26.9	39.5	55.7	76.3	101.7
Unspecified: Engineers	M	34.5	14.5	35.1	73.2	146.2
& firemen, mechanics,	F	13.3	—	8.1	34.3	22.7
machine minders &	A	47.8	14.5	43.2	107.5	168.9
unspecified manufacture						

		1841	1851	1861	1871	1881
F. *Transport*						
Navigation & docks (not	M	114.4	263.9	302.4	340.9	379.3
seamen abroad)	F	1.3	10.2	7.3	12.5	9.3
	A	115.7	274.1	309.7	353.4	388.6
Railways	M	2.3	28.7	60.3	96.5	157.3
	F	—	0.1	0.1	0.3	0.8
	A	2.3	28.8	60.4	96.8	158.1
Roads	M	53.7	87.3	119.3	143.1	190.9
	F	1.5	2.5	2.9	2.9	1.5
	A	55.2	89.8	122.2	146.0	192.4
G. *Dealing*						
Raw materials	M	25.2	42.6	57.7	75.9	66.1
	F	1.7	1.3	4.3	6.1	3.2
	A	26.9	43.9	62.0	82.0	69.3
Clothing materials &	M	38.1	51.6	75.3	79.1	85.4
dress	F	4.7	9.9	18.7	26.9	39.5
	A	42.8	61.5	94.0	106.0	124.9
Food, drink & smoking	M	172.7	267.2	300.7	356.7	395.5
	F	33.3	55.9	69.7	77.9	84.0
	A	206.0	323.1	370.4	434.6	479.5
Lodging & coffee houses	M	2.5	6.3	6.5	7.6	10.5
	F	9.3	21.9	23.2	32.9	41.1
	A	11.8	28.2	29.7	40.5	51.6
Furniture, utensils &	M	26.6	39.4	54.2	65.3	77.5
stationery	F	2.9	5.6	9.2	12.8	17.8
	A	29.5	45.0	63.4	78.1	95.3
General dealers &	M	65.2	84.6	105.3	145.0	168.3
unspecified	F	17.6	34.8	37.8	58.3	58.0
	A	82.8	119.4	143.1	203.3	226.3
H. *Industrial service*						
Commercial	M	48.0	52.2	77.7	135.7	251.0
	F	0.2	0.1	0.5	2.0	7.9
	A	48.2	52.3	78.2	137.7	258.9
General labour	M	345.5	365.3	348.3	556.5	623.8
	F	14.5	8.9	4.7	8.7	3.8
	A	360.0	374.2	353.0	565.2	627.6
I. *Public service & professional*						
Administration	M	23.4	55.6	67.5	75.7	81.6
	F	1.0	2.5	4.1	6.5	10.2
	A	24.4	58.1	71.6	82.2	91.8
Army & navy, exc.	M	51.8	94.3	141.9	144.8	132.8
those abroad. Up to	F	—	—	—	—	—
1871, inc. artificers	A	51.8	94.3	141.9	144.8	132.8
& labourers in govt						
dockyards. In 1881,						
these were transferred						
to their trades.						

		1841	*1851*	*1861*	*1871*	*1881*
Police & prisons	M	15.1	18.3	27.5	34.9	39.5
	F	—	—	0.7	0.8	0.7
	A	15.1	18.3	28.2	35.7	40.2
Law	M	34.1	37.5	39.0	44.4	50.3
	F	—	—	—	—	0.1
	A	34.1	37.5	39.0	44.4	50.4
Medicine	M	31.6	38.2	40.8	46.3	52.1
	F	16.6	28.7	29.6	33.7	41.1
	A	48.2	66.9	70.4	80.0	93.2
Art & amusement	M	15.8	25.6	27.3	34.4	38.8
	F	1.0	2.8	4.2	6.9	12.4
	A	16.8	28.4	31.5	41.3	51.2
Literature & science	M	0.8	2.2	3.5	6.7	8.9
	F	—	—	0.3	0.3	0.5
	A	0.8	2.2	3.8	7.0	9.4
Education	M	26.1	34.1	40.1	42.8	59.2
	F	33.2	71.3	89.2	105.8	143.0
	A	59.3	105.4	129.3	148.6	202.2
Religion	M	23.4	34.3	40.9	44.6	50.0
	F	—	0.9	3.4	5.7	7.7
	A	23.4	35.2	44.3	50.3	57.7
J. *Domestic service*						
Indoor	M	228.8	105.0	96.0	110.2	106.5
	F	885.6	899.1	1117.5	1361.2	1404.7
	A	1114.4	1004.1	1213.5	1471.4	1511.2
Outdoor: in the	M	10.4	38.3	66.1	81.3	185.6
census, public and	F	0.4	—	1.0	1.2	1.2
private coachmen,	A	10.8	38.3	67.1	82.5	186.8
and domestic and						
market gardeners						
confused. 1881						
figures exaggerated						
or earlier ones						
understated.						
Extra	M	16.1	18.3	21.4	24.9	31.2
	F	71.8	198.5	246.8	264.4	291.6
	A	87.9	216.8	268.2	289.3	322.8
K. *Indefinite*						
Presumably occupation	M	384.8	113.1	92.6	138.6	284.1
not described	F	—	—	—	—	—
	A	384.8	113.1	92.6	138.6	284.1
Grand total	M	4524.5	6688.6	7368.8	8201.8	9163.6
	F	1807.4	2816.8	3240.1	3654.7	3887.2
	A	7231.9	9505.4	10608.9	11856.5	13050.8

1.2   THE OCCUPATIONS OF THE PEOPLE CONSIDERED

In examining the returns for the different divisions of the kingdom, it must be premised that, owing to the different method of tabulation as to ages and the imperfections of the returns, the figures for 1841 do not, so far as England and Scotland are concerned, offer a very safe basis for comparison, and have not therefore been used in this paper. They are, however, given in the tables, while the incomplete ones for 1831 also appear in the more detailed tables, a copy of which is deposited in the library of the Statistical Society.

England and Wales

Between 1851 and 1881 the whole population increased 12 per cent in the first decade, 13 per cent in the second, and 14¼ per cent in the third. At the same time the dependent women and children (those not returned as employed in any way) increased from 53 per cent of the whole population in 1851 to 55 per cent in 1881, almost the whole of this increase lying with the children. The employment of girls under the age of 15 was as follows:

1851	205 000
1861	224 000
1871	254 000
1881	210 000.

Their main fields of employment were the textile industries and domestic service. Table [1.2] shows the distribution of female workers over 15.

Between 1851 and 1871, the proportion of women industrially employed declined, while those in education and domestic service rose, a pattern repeated for the whole occupied or self-supporting class. Between 1851 and 1881, the proportion engaged in productive or distributive industry fell from 78.4 per cent to 74.2 per cent, while there was an increase in the service sectors:

	1851	*1881*
Percentage employed in:		
Public and Professional Service	4.6	5.6
Domestic Service	13.3	15.7

Table 1.2   Changes in the employment of women aged over 15, England and Wales, 1851–81 (in thousands)

Occupations	1851		1861		1871		1881	
	Nos	%	Nos	%	Nos	%	Nos	%
Textiles, etc.	391	16.7	443	16.3	466	14.9	500	14.7
Dress	441	18.8	525	19.4	529	17.0	589	17.4
Others	358	15.2	364	13.4	434	13.9	465	13.7
Industry, total	1190	50.7	1332	49.1	1429	45.8	1554	45.8
Medicine	26	1.1	27	1.0	31	1.0	38	1.1
Education	67	2.8	82	3.0	97	3.1	127	3.7
Domestic service	909	38.7	1128	41.6	1375	44.1	1446	42.6
Others	6	0.3	11	0.4	18	0.6	28	0.8
Independent	150	6.4	130	4.8	168	5.4	200	5.9
Total self-supporting	2348	100	2710	100	3118	100	3393	100

With regard to Domestic Service, it is noteworthy that the increase lies mainly in the women and girls, the indoor men servants having decreased from 74 000 in 1851 to 56 000 in 1881, while the population has risen from 18 to 26 millions – a fact that would seem to indicate a greater diffusion of wealth, and also, perhaps, less ostentation of expenditure of the very rich. On the other hand, the number of public and private coachmen has more than doubled:

1851	43 100
1881	103 700.

Table [1.3] analyses these changes by occupational group. This picture separates the industrial classes into three main divisions, showing the percentage of those engaged in or supported by (1) the production of raw materials, (2) the preparing them for use, and (3) distributing productions finished and unfinished, and it will be at once observed how enormous are the interests of production and manufacture compared with those of distribution, so far as they can rightly be separated at all.

Coming now to a detailed review of the industrial classes, we notice, first, that the production of raw material employs a decreasing percentage. We depend, as is well enough known, more on what we import, and less on what we find at home. The reduction, however, falls entirely on Agriculture, as the percentage in Fishing and Mining have increased. And it is to the present condition of Agriculture that more attention has lately been given than to any other part of our

Table 1.3 Employments of the people by percentage, England and Wales, 1851–81 (sub-totals in brackets)

Occupations	1851		1861		1871		1881	
Agriculture	20.9		18.0		14.2		11.5	
Fishing	0.2		0.2		0.2		0.3	
Mining	4.0	(25.1)	4.5	(22.7)	4.5	(18.9)	4.8	(16.6)
Building	5.5		5.8		6.3		6.8	
Manufacture	32.7	(38.2)	33.0	(38.8)	31.6	(37.9)	30.7	(37.5)
Transport	4.1		4.6		4.9		5.6	
Dealing	6.5	(10.6)	7.1	(11.7)	7.3	(12.7)	7.8	(13.4)
Industrial service		(4.5)		(4.0)		(6.0)		(6.7)
Industry		78.4		77.2		75.5		74.2
Public and professional service	4.6		5.3		5.5		5.6	
Domestic service	13.3		14.6		15.8		15.7	
Others	3.7	(21.6)	2.9	(22.8)	3.2	(24.5)	4.4[a]	(25.8)
Occupied population		100.0		100.0		100.0		100.0

[a]The figures here are subject to correction of about 1 per cent for retired persons previously included with their nominal trades.

industrial position. We have to face the fact that for the three decades since 1851, those employed on the land have decreased by 419 000, or 26 per cent. At the same time it is somewhat singular that in 1841 there were fewer persons employed on the land than at present: 1 297 000 against 1 341 000. The returns for 1841 cannot be trusted implicitly; nevertheless it is certain that a great increase (amounting according to these returns to 462 000) must have taken place in the agricultural population between 1841 and 1851. The increase is largely in the numbers of young males and females, suggesting that they were under-counted in 1841 or over-counted in 1851, or else that so great was the impetus given to this industry during the ten years in question, that all the available members of the labourer's family were for the first time pressed into active employment on the land.

Against the losses that followed 1851, mostly in ordinary agricultural labour, must be set the equivalent of the increased use of machinery, before we can say that less energy is devoted to the cultivation of the soil now than thirty years ago. A new class connected with the application of science to agriculture has sprung into being, that points to a change of system, involving improvements, rather than neglect of any kind, as a cause of the decrease in the agricultural population.

Table 1.4   Increase of population, with changes in numbers supported by agriculture, England and Wales, 1801–81 (in thousands)

Year	Population	Increase		Total supported by agriculture	
		Nos	*%*	*Nos*	*%*
1801	8 893	—	—	1713	19
1811	10 164	1271	$14\frac{1}{4}$	2695	$26\frac{1}{2}$
1821	12 000	1836	18	2698	$22\frac{1}{2}$
1831	13 897	1897	$15\frac{3}{4}$	2923	21
1841	15 912	2015	$14\frac{1}{2}$	3875	24
1851[a]	17 928	2016	$12\frac{2}{3}$	4247	24
1861	20 066	2138	12	4194	21
1871	22 712	2647	13	3746	$16\frac{1}{2}$
1881	25 974	3261	$14\frac{1}{4}$	3435	13

[a] About 400 000 persons are stated to have come to England from Ireland, and settled in England, between 1841 and 1851.

The facts as given in the census returns show us that in the last thirty years England has changed from a population about half agricultural and half manufacturing, to one in which Manufacture is double of Agriculture, and we have no reason to suppose that the process of change in this direction is yet ended. This change has been accompanied by an enormous increase in the total population, so that, altogether, support has been found during this period, in other ways than the tilling of the soil, for a new population of 8½ million souls. In this immense figure, those who have failed to obtain subsistence from Agriculture are completely swallowed up.

To state this question more fully, we may go back to the beginning of the present century. Table [1.4] shows that since that time we have had to find new means of support for no fewer than 17 millions of people. In the returns of 1811, 1821, and 1831, only the number of families supported by Agriculture is given, not the number of individuals. For those years I have reckoned 3½ individuals to a family, rather less than the proportion for the whole population.

It would thus seem, from such figures as we have, that of the total increase of 17 millions, some 2 or 2½ millions had up to 1851 been provided for on the land, but that, of these, ¾ million have been since transferred to other industries. How the great bulk of these millions have been provided for, while the numbers supported by Agriculture have remained comparatively so constant, is the question, and whether the process can continue. The yearly increase of population now is greater than ever; can we expect to provide for the additional millions of the future in the same ways, or must some other means be found?

Our picture of what has happened would be much more complete if we could go back to 1801, but we can only do this by drawing largely upon the imagination. We know that Manufacture was then an adjunct of Agriculture, and that a hundred things were made at home for which everyone now goes to a shop; we know that machinery and commerce have changed this, and we see the end of the period of revolution in the amazing figures of change between 1841 and 1851, when the furthest point of unrestricted competition was reached, and when the reaction towards socialism commenced with the Factory Acts; but it is only of the period since 1851 that the census figures enable us to speak with any accuracy.

We come now to the second branch of the production of raw material, *Fishing*, which has prospered considerably. The whole numbers involved are not large, but those employed have increased 77 per cent, or twice as fast as the total occupied population. The increased numbers employed in this way count up to 13 000, and there seems to be no reason why progress in this direction should stop short; on the contrary, a better organisation of the distribution of fish might largely increase the scope of the trade, and it is encouraging to see the good results of the last decade.

Mining, which has also prospered, has increased 68 per cent during the thirty years, against an increase of 39 per cent in the total employed population. The total numbers are large, those engaged in this industry in 1881 being 227 000 more than in 1851. Nine-tenths of this increase is due to coal; copper and lead mining have greatly fallen off, and tin has decreased slightly. Iron shows a moderate increase, and the rest is made up of quarrying and brick making, which are included in the same class, and which both show a large increase. The decrease lies in metals of such value as can admit of carriage from places at a distance, where they are dug up more readily than in England; the increase lies in those of so low a value compared to bulk that the cost of carriage provides a natural protection.

Quarrying and brick making may be expected to grow with the general prosperity. It is as to the coal trade that serious questions arise. The output has enormously increased from about 50 million tons in 1851, to about 130 millions in 1881, while those employed in raising it have also more than doubled in number. Little comparatively is exported for sale, the greater part being used at home or burnt by outward bound steamers, and it is to a continuously growing consumption in these ways that we have to look.

We now come to the backbone of the industrial organism we are studying, namely Building and Manufacture, which I venture to bracket as being alike the turning of raw materials into things serviceable, and we find that this remains nearly constant at 38 per cent of the employed population.

The numbers engaged in *Building* have increased 73 per cent, as against 39 per cent for the whole employed population, the addition to the total being 335 000, and well maintained up to 1881.

Manufactures, taken as a whole, have increased in the thirty years 30½ per cent, or 8½ less than the whole employed population, and this comparative falling off is progressive. Nevertheless we have here found support for about 2 millions out of the 8½ millions for which, in all, fresh means of support have been obtained since 1851, whilst the deficiency in proportion to population has been nearly made good by the increasing proportion employed in Building. It must not be forgotten also that, measured by production, our manufacturing energy has increased far beyond the increase of the whole population, and some economic mal-adjustment may be fairly assumed if the community generally can be shown not to share in the benefit.

Looking into the various sections of Manufacture, we shall not be surprised to find a great increase in those engaged in the construction of machinery and tools, which has risen from 1.2 per cent of the employed population in 1851 to 1.9 per cent in 1881, or in numbers from 100 000 to 224 000. Metal workers have similarly gone up from 293 000 to 477 000 (or 63 per cent), the iron and steel trades having doubled their numbers. Smaller branches, like the earthenware, coal, gas, chemical, paper, floor cloth and waterproof manufactures, have all kept pace with the growth of population, and have in some cases increased 100 to 150 per cent. It is in the greatest of all our manufactures, the textile industries, that the decreasing proportion as compared to population shows itself. In 1851 these industries with their natural ally, dyeing, found work for 11.1 per cent of our workers, but in 1881 only 8.1 per cent were so employed. As regards actual numbers there was an increase of 27000 or 2.9 per cent. Taking the cotton trade by itself, we find the increase has not been far behind that for the whole occupied population, 31 per cent as against 39 per cent, but silk on the other hand shows a decided decline of more than 50 per cent, operating steadily over the whole period. The workers in woollen fabrics have also decreased upon the whole, but the figures show a peculiar variation:

1851	258 000
1861	229 000
1871	245 000
1881	234 000

Flax and linen manufacture has strikingly fallen off from 26 000 to 12 000, and is insufficiently compensated by the increase in hemp and jute. Some consolation may be obtained, however, by noting the flourishing condition of these industries in Scotland.

The workers in dress have increased in number by 85 000 during the thirty years, but nevertheless the proportion to population is less than in 1851. The cause of these comparative decreases is to be found in the greatly increased use of machinery, which is witnessed by the figures of the unspecified section of manufacture (consisting mainly of the 'workers of machinery', who did not specify the trade for which their machinery was used, perhaps only as the driving power), which has risen from 13 000 to 142 000, or from 0.2 per cent to 1.2 per cent of the employed population. This increase may perhaps largely be set against the decrease in textiles and dress.

Food, drink, and smoking remain constant at 1.6 per cent of the employed; and those branches of mechanics most nearly connected with art, as watch and instrument making, printing and bookbinding, show large increases.

The third division of Industry comprises those engaged in the distribution of merchandise (finished or otherwise), and has two branches, called here Transport and Dealing.

Transport (which includes also all forms of travel) has increased enormously. In 1851 this industry employed 345 000 persons; in 1881 the figures had risen to 654 000, or by nearly 90 per cent. The analysis of this class points to changes in the methods and possibilities of industry which would repay separate study. As might have been expected, the greatest increase is in the railway employés, from 25 000 to 139 000, but navigation and docks have fully kept pace with the advance of population. Most remarkable, therefore, under the circumstances, is the very large increase of persons engaged in conveyance by road. Side by side with the gigantic strides which railways have made, there has been an addition of 195 000, or 60 per cent, to the numbers engaged in other forms of transport. Of this increase road conveyance claims 94 000, or an advance of 127 per cent on the numbers of 1851. The number of those properly in this class who have called themselves *private servants* are not included here, and if added would make the figure still more striking.

Dealing has increased 69 per cent, as against the 39 per cent increase of the total occupied population, a change due largely to the multiplication of small shopkeepers and street sellers. The actual numbers are:

1851	547 000
1881	924 000

The increase is very regular for the several decades. It should be stated, however, that it was in not a few cases impossible to separate accurately the dealers from the manufacturers. This however will have had but very little effect on the comparative percentages, as the possibility of error lies in small compass.

The last division of Industry, called here *Industrial Service*, ought not properly speaking to contain any besides those engaged in banking, insurance and accounts, but the returns of labour are so made and arranged that I have had to include with them in the same division (though under a separate heading) all general labour, or labour not allotted to any particular trade, and of this class of labour there was a remarkable increase between 1861 and 1871; but the returns are not to be trusted entirely, and the most we can say is that a low class of more or less casual labour appears to have increased since 1861 beyond the average increase of the population. Information on this subject would be very valuable, but it is not to be found in the census returns, where skilled and common labour are inextricably confused. The other section covers all commercial clerks, accountants and bankers; and the great and continuous increase here points even more forcibly than is the case with transport to a revolution in the method and management of industry, the effect of which must be far beyond the single fact we are now noticing:

1851	44 000
1861	67 000
1871	119 000
1881	225 000

Note, though, that the increase in the last decade is partly due to a change in the method of enumeration.

The labour section may be taken as devoted mainly to the service of Building, Manufacture and Transport, as Dealing affords little employment for common labour, and Agriculture, Fishing and Mining return their own; but every class of industry shares in the benefit of the commercial system maintained by bankers, accountants and clerks.

The picture we have now completed of the industrial development of England since 1851 and her apparent position in 1881 is, on the whole, one which may be regarded with satisfaction. Nor could any changes since 1881 seriously affect this result. Every line of it shows vitality, and an innate power of meeting changes of circumstances, which seem to give promise of continued prosperity.

Scotland

The growth of the population of Scotland (6¾, 9¾, and 11½ per cent for the three decades) has been slower than that of England, and the proportions engaged in each of the main divisions of industry are somewhat different, but the points of similarity are much more noticeable than the points of difference, as is shown in Table 1.5. We see a similar falling off in the proportion connected with Agriculture, a similar constancy in those connected with Building and Manufacture, and a similar increase under other heads.

Table 1.5   Employments of the people by percentage, Scotland, 1851–81 (sub-totals in brackets)

Occupations	1851		1861		1871		1881	
Agriculture, etc.	22.7		20.1		17.3		14.2	
Fishing	1.5		1.7		1.8		1.9	
Mining	4.0	(28.2)	4.5	(26.3)	5.1	(24.2)	5.0	(21.1)
Building	5.2		5.9		6.3		6.7	
Manufacture	36.5	(41.7)	35.0	(40.9)	34.7	(41.0)	33.8	(40.5)
Transport	3.6		4.1		4.9		5.2	
Dealing	5.6	(9.2)	6.5	(10.6)	7.1	(12.0)	7.5	(12.7)
Industrial service	—	(3.8)	—	(3.9)	—	(4.5)	—	(6.2)
Industry		82.9		81.7		81.7		80.5
Public and professional service	3.5		3.9		3.8		4.2	
Domestic service	10.5		12.0		10.7		11.1	
Others	3.1	(17.1)	2.4	(18.3)	3.8	(18.3)	4.2	(19.5)
		100.0		100.0		100.0		100.0

The minor similarities are also very noticeable, and although the figures for the respective countries may provide materials for many interesting inquiries, either of special interest to Scotland, or of comparison between England and Scotland, it is unnecessary to pursue them here. The figures show that the two countries share each other's fortune, and make the union of feeling between them easy to understand.

2 1881–1911

Booth surveyed the re-creation of the Britain of his day and was well satisfied. Seventeen million additional people had been provided for, while the numbers engaged in agriculture had remained comparatively constant. But, he asked a little anxiously, could the process continue? We are now in a position to see whether his satisfaction was well based, and his anxiety unnecessary.

The rate of railway expansion was decelerating. Between 1841 and 1871, miles added averaged 3871 per decade. In the decade to 1881, 2346 miles were added; the figures for the following decades were:

1881–91	1594 miles
1891–1901	1542 miles
1901–11	1145 miles (see Mitchell and Deane, 1962, pp. 225–7)

But while the railway transformation matured, the steel transformation erupted. The Bessemer was followed by the open-hearth process, enabling the mass production of cheap steel. Output rose from 329 000 tons in 1871 to 3 157 000 tons in 1891 and 6 262 000 in 1911 (Mitchell and Deane, 1962, pp. 136–7).

Table 2.1 takes up the story where Chapter 1 left off. Massive increases in population continued, each decade was called upon to provide an additional 1¾ million jobs (2 million in the decade to 1911) and, within the limits of the trade cycle, succeeding in doing so. In the first half of the nineteenth century, employment in agriculture rose by a factor of 2½. But between 1851 and 1881, it declined by one-fifth. Booth remarked on the increased use of machinery, and the appearance of a new class concerned with the application of science to agriculture. A rise in numbers between 1901 and 1911 was still less than that in the occupied population: in 1881, 12.8 per cent had been employed in agriculture; in 1911 only 8.2 per cent.

The decline of employment in agriculture and its advance in manufacturing are key indexes of modernisation, in which Britain set the pattern for the rest of the world.

Figure 2.1 illustrates the changes that were in train: a shift from agriculture and domestic service to manufacture, transport, mining and a number of lesser sectors. In some ways, 'professionals and subordinate services' hold the key for what is to come, for it is the

Table 2.1 Analysis of the occupied population, Great Britain, 1881–1911 (in thousands)

	1881 Nos	1881 %	1891 Nos	1891 %	1901 Nos	1901 %	1911 Nos	1911 %
Public administration	118	0.9	163	1.1	220	1.4	321	1.8
Armed forces	114	0.9	134	0.9	176	1.1	221	1.2
Professionals and subordinate services	457	3.6	551	3.8	674	4.1	796	4.3
Domestic and personal service	1994	15.7	2329	16.1	2344	14.4	2583	14.1
Commerce and finance	363	2.9	475	3.3	673	4.1	896	4.9
Transport and communication	885	6.9	1124	7.7	1436	8.8	1609	8.8
Agriculture	1633	12.8	1502	10.4	1406	8.6	1496	8.2
Fishing	61	0.5	54	0.4	51	0.3	53	0.3
Mining, quarrying and working in their products	612	4.8	758	5.2	937	5.8	1210	6.6
Building and construction	877	6.9	902	6.2	1219	7.5	1145	6.3
Manufacture	4664	36.6	5368	37.0	6130	37.6	7031	38.4
Gas, electricity, water	24	0.2	38	0.3	62	0.4	86	0.5
All others	932	7.3	1098	7.6	962	5.9	839	4.6
Total occupied	12734	100	14499	100	16280	100	18286	100

Source: Department of Employment, *British Labour Statistics Historical Abstract 1886–1968* (HMSO, 1971), Table 102, p. 195. For primary sources, see text.

'workers by brain' who educate the 'workers by hand', and create the blue-prints for the future. Their numbers rise from 457 000 to 796 000, and their proportion in the labour forces rises from 3.6 to 4.3 per cent. It is a rise of less than one percentage point, but a percentage point in 1911 equalled 182 000 people.

Figure 2.1   Distribution of employment by occupational order, Great Britain, 1811–1911

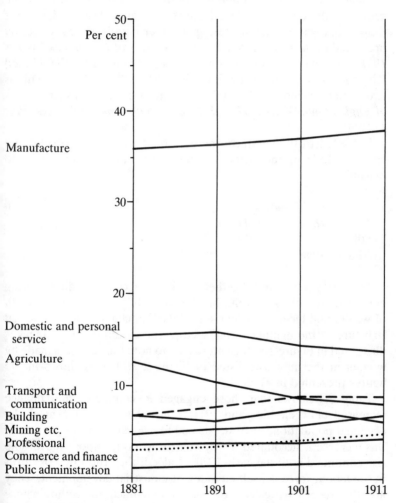

Source: as Table 2.1.

Building is a most volatile industry, rising and falling with the trade cycle, so its numbers and proportions fall between 1901 and 1911. Transport and communication continue their advance, though between 1901 and 1911 their increase in numbers employed is just equal in proportion to that of the whole labour force. Public administration, commerce and finance continue their inexorable advance, since all are engaged in servicing the expansion of industry by maintenance, supervision and promotion.

Table 102 of *British Labour Statistics 1886–1968*, which is the source of the data in Table 2.1, gives a breakdown by industry for those employed in manufacturing. Further details are conveniently presented in the *General Report* of the *Census of England and Wales 1901*. This gives data for persons, males and females for the 'United Kingdom and its three divisions' in 1881, 1891 and 1901. This is extended to include 1911, but for England and Wales only, in *Census of England and Wales 1911, vol. X, Occupations and Industries, Part I*, Table 64.

In 1881, British manufacturing was still dominated by textiles and clothing. Indeed, employment in these two industries continued to expand:

	000s	
	1881	*1911*
Textiles	1221	1464
Clothing	1046	1257.

In 1881 they accounted together for 48.6 per cent of manufacturing employment, but by 1911 this had fallen to 38.7 per cent. The growth of wealth and technology manifested itself in changes in the internal structure of the manufacturing sector. The extent of the changes is illustrated in Figure 2.2. It is interesting to note the advances made by women in the industries listed in Figure 2.2. This is shown in the figures presented in Table 2.2.

Table 2.1 shows that those engaged in commerce and finance increased between 1881 and 1911 from 2.9 to 4.9 per cent of the occupied population, or from 363 000 to 896 000. A large portion of this increase is accounted for by clerical workers, whose inexorable rise continued until the early 1970s. Indeed, the proportion of clerks in the labour force is itself an index of industrial development. They are the recorders, calculators and communicators within whose ambience the decision-makers make their decisions, lenders lend,

Figure 2.2   Distribution of employment within manufacturing industry, Great Britain, 1881–1911

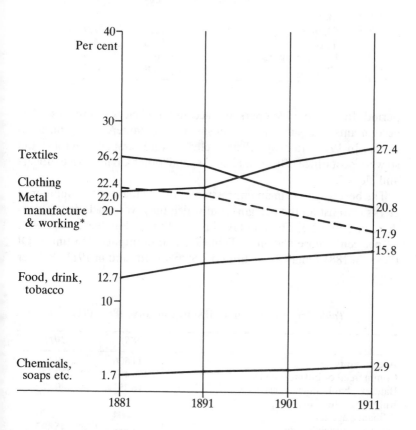

*Metal manufacture and working includes iron and steel, machines, implements and vehicles.

Source: As Table 2.1.

borrowers borrow and, in due course, repay, and administrators administer. The more these things are done, the more clerks are required to do them. A side-effect, of considerable social import-ance, was the disproportionate rise in the numbers of female clerks.

In 1881, the census for England and Wales distinguished 181 457 'commercial or business clerks'; by 1911 their number had risen to 477 535. Females constituted 3.3 per cent in 1881, and 24.5 per cent in 1911. But census divisions and definitions had changed over the

Table 2.2   Women as % of labour force, 1881–1911

	1881	*1911*
Metals	4.8	6.7
Chemicals	11.1	22.9
Textiles	54.6	56.4
Food, drink, tobacco	16.6	27.6
Clothing	63.8	65.6

period. In 1881 bookkeepers and accountants' clerks were classed as accountants, in subsequent censuses as commercial or business clerks. In 1911, 'railway officials, clerks' were lumped together, and so were post office officers and clerks, and 'other Civil Service officers and clerks'.

The best way to gain an impression of the increase in the number of clerks is to list all the categories in which they were included. This is done in Table 2.3. The employed population had increased by about 44 per cent; those shown in Table 2.3 had multiplied 3½ times. Of these, in 1881 females constituted 2.85 per cent, and in 1911 18.2 per cent.

Table 2.3   Increase in clerks, by category, 1881–1911

	1881	*1911*
Accountants	11606	9499
Commercial or business clerks	181457	477535
Bankers, bank officials, clerks	16055	40379
Bill-discounters, brokers, finance agents	604	3570
Insurance officials, clerks	} 15068	45897
Insurance agents		54031
Railway officials, clerks	—	85922
PO officers and clerks	—	50210
Other Civil Service officers and clerks	—	33037
All	224790	800080

3 1911–1951

3.1 OCCUPATIONAL CLASSES

In 1911, as has been noted, a first attempt was made to produce separate tables for distributions by occupation and by industry. Inspired by the British Empire Statistical Conference of 1920, the Registrar General and his Officials repeated this endeavour in a more determined way in 1921, so that the ambiguity that bedevilled previous reports was largely removed. So it is that it becomes possible to mobilise workers into occupational classes defined by characteristics inherent in their occupations. This is what I have done with the census data from 1911 to 1981, in an endeavour to measure the quality of the labour force. The occupational classes used here are related to, and generally derived from, the social classes and socio-economic groups used in the census (see *Census 1951: Classifiation of Occupations*, HMSO, 1956; and Routh, 1965, Appendix A).

The 584 occupations distinguished in the census of 1951 were posted to seven classes, two of which were subdivided:

Occupational Class 1A Higher professional
1B Lower professional
2A Employers and proprietors
2B Managers and administrators
3 Clerical workers
4 Foremen, inspectors, supervisors
5 Skilled manual workers
6 Semi-skilled manual workers
7 Unskilled manual workers

For the convenience of those who wish to update the analysis to 1991 (and beyond?), the Appendix on p. 89 shows the allocation of 1981 census occupations to occupational classes. The best way of discovering the scope of each class is to study the Appendix, but as a quick guide the following notes may be used.

The higher professions (Class 1A, or the 'learned professions' as they have traditionally been called) include those occupations that require some years of study for their acquisition at universities or institutions of similar nature. Included are all the occupations in the

Registrar General's Social Class I *except* those who are there in the capacity of managers or administrators.

The lower professions (Class 1B) are from the Registrar General's Social Class II: artists, draughtsmen, librarians, medical auxiliaries, officials of associations, pharmacists and teachers. But some are also included from Social Class III: actors, aircrew, musicians and professional sportsmen.

Employers and proprietors (Class 2A) include *all* employers except those in the higher or lower professions whose professional qualification is given precedence over their status as employer. The proprietors are the owners of non-incorporated businesses who have no employees but for which the ownership of property is decisive. Thus farmers, shopkeepers and boarding-house proprietors are included, while window cleaners, building craftsmen and tailors working on their own account are not.

Administrators and managers (Class 2B) include managers in service and production industries and administrators and other higher officers in the public service.

Clerical workers (Class 3) are those engaged in paper-work (or its computerised equivalent) and include costing, estimating and accounting clerks, bookkeepers (not qualified accountants), insurance agents and canvassers, office machine operators, typists and shorthand typists.

Foremen, supervisors, inspectors (Class 4) are in charge of groups of workers, their responsibility being to see that defined tasks are properly done. They include inspectors, viewers, testers, farm bailiffs and coalmining overmen. But clerical workers who supervise clerks are allocated to Class 3, and supervisors who are professional workers to Classes 1A or 1B.

Skilled manual workers (Class 5) are craftsmen who have served their apprenticeship and have thereby acquired theoretical knowledge that backs up their ability to handle materials, instruments and machines. Since the Second World War, the requirement of apprenticeship has to some extent been relaxed, so that those who have acquired the necessary skills on-the-job or in government training centres may be admitted to craft status. There are also some trades in which the status of skilled worker is achieved without formal apprenticeship but through experience and promotion, the principal being the steel industry and coalmining.

Semi-skilled manual workers (Class 6) perform tasks that can be learnt in months rather than years. They include machine operators or assemblers in the process of production, ticket collectors and conductors, vehicle drivers, postmen and sorters, telephone operators, waiters, domestic servants, shop assistants and agricultural workers.

Unskilled manual workers (Class 7) do jobs that can be learnt in hours rather than months. They include labourers in various industries who require strength and stamina rather than skill. Included here are charwomen and office cleaners, door-keepers, porters and watchmen.

The census authorities consult employers and trade unionists as well as officials from other government departments when they determine their lists of occupations and their allocation to social classes and socio-economic groups. Within firms and industries, the skill-rating of specific jobs is often the subject of collective bargaining, for this determines the wage band within which the relevant workers are paid. Elaborate systems of job evaluation are frequently employed to add an element of objectivity to the process, but there remain important elements of judgement and opinion. In the United States, postmen and shop assistants are classified as white-collar (or non-manual) workers, with shop assistants being called sales clerks. In Britain, the problem has been avoided by a multiplication of socio-economic groups, with shop assistants given a group of their own.

3.2 OCCUPATIONAL CLASS STRUCTURE, 1911–51

In the census of 1921, the distinction between occupational and industrial classification was at last clearly drawn and subsequently maintained. This has made it possible to marshall the occupied population by occupational class with a degree of consistency that allows for inter-census comparisons. For 1911, however, the task was by no means easy. For the professions and the building industry, demarcations in the census were similar to those subsequently applied; for mining and the railways, occupational data were available from contemporary reports produced by the industries themselves; for process and maintenance workers in manufacturing industry, where occupational and industrial features were confused, the census data were unscrambled according to the occupational distribution shown, for each industry, by the Board of Trade earnings and hours reports, published in eight parts between 1909 and 1913. The results of these manipulations are shown in Table 3.1.

Table 3.1	Occupied population by occupational class, Great Britain, 1911, 1921, 1931, 1951 (in thousands)

			1911	1921	1931	1951
1A	Higher professions		184	195	240	434
		%	1.00	1.01	1.14	1.93
1B	Lower professions		560	680	728	1059
		%	3.05	3.52	3.46	4.70
2A	Employers and proprietors		1232	1318	1409	1118
		%	6.71	6.82	6.70	4.97
2B	Managers and administrators		629	704	770	1246
		%	3.43	3.64	3.66	5.53
3	Clerical workers		887	1300	1465	2404
		%	4.84	6.72	6.97	10.68
4	Foremen, inspectors, supervisors		236	279	323	590
		%	1.29	1.44	1.54	2.62
5	Skilled manual workers		5608	5573	5619	5616
		%	30.56	28.83	26.72	24.95
6	Semi-skilled manual workers		7244	6544	7360	7338
		%	39.48	33.85	35.00	32.60
7	Unskilled manual workers		1767	2740	3115	2709
		%	9.63	14.17	14.81	12.03
	All		18347	19333	21029	22514
		%	100.00	100.00	100.00	100.00
	All as % of previous total		—	105.37	108.77	107.26

Source: Routh, 1965, pp. 4 and 5.

What can we learn from this table about the social history of Britain? We are surely entitled to expect great qualitative changes in the constitution of the labour force, following two world wars, a great depression, the eclipse of the great textile industry, the rise of the electrical and chemical industries, the substitution of the internal combustion engine for horses and steam, the advent of the airliner and telecommunications, and the proliferation of household durables. Yet the preponderance of the blue-collared proletariat remains. Foremen and manual workers formed 81 per cent of the labour force in 1911 and 72 per cent in 1951. The absolute number of skilled and semi-skilled workers hardly changed, though unskilled workers increased by 50 per cent and foremen and supervisors by a factor of 2½.

Numbers in Class 2 (employers, proprietors, managers and administrators) rose a little more than those for all workers, so that they constituted 10.14 per cent of the total in 1911 and 10.5 per cent in

1951. The profound changes in industry and production appear to have manifested themselves in large changes in the smallest classes: the doubling in the number of professionals and the more-than-doubling of foremen and clerks:

	1951 as % of 1911	
1A Higher professional	235.9	200.7
1B Lower professional	189.1	
2A Employers and proprietors	90.7	127.0
2B Managers and administrators	198.1	
3 Clerical workers	271.0	
4 Foremen, inspectors, supervisors	250.0	
5 Skilled manual workers	100.1	107.1
6 Semi-skilled manual workers	101.3	
7 Unskilled workers	153.3	
All	122.7	

3.3 THE INCIDENCE OF CHANGE

Let us look first at that revealing index of social change, the participation rate for women. Women were enfranchised in the United Kingdom in 1918, but this had little effect on their employment:

	%	
	1911	*1951*
Females aged 14 and over in employment, 1911	35.3	
Females aged 15 and over in employment, 1951		34.0
Females as proportion of labour force	29.6	30.8

After 1951, there was a substantial increase in both proportions, but we shall consider this in the next chapter.

Within the stability of those proportions, there were considerable shifts between occupational classes. Between 1911 and 1951, the female labour force increased by 1 505 000, allocated between the classes as follows:

	000s
Professional A	+25
Professional B	+215
Employers, proprietors	−9
Managers, administrators	+64
Clerical	+1235
Forewomen, inspectors, supervisors	+69
Skilled manual	−460
Semi skilled manual	+90
Unskilled manual	+276
All	+1505

The role of women in the labour force remains one of subservience. Professional B is, in important respects, subservient to Professional A; Classes 3 to 7 are subservient to Class 2B; Classes 5, 6 and 7 are subservient to Class 4, and Class 3 serves or subserves all the others. Thus of every 1000 sub-professionals 535 were women, but only 83 in the case of Professional A. Among clerical workers, 589 per thousand were women, but among managers only 152 and among foremen/women only 134.

Changes within classes

Higher professions

It was only among churchmen or -women that numbers fell absolutely between 1911 and 1951, and only in the law that they fell relative to the total employed. The number of accountants and commissioned officers more than tripled, engineers increased by a factor of 5½, and scientists by a factor of almost 10. But there were still only 49 000 scientists in 1951, and 138 000 engineers, surveyors and architects.

Lower professions

In 1951 five occupations accounted for 80 per cent of this class:

	000s
Nurses	266
Subordinate medical services	52
Teachers	340
Draughtsmen	130
Lab technicians	69

In 1911, the census included draughtsmen with clerks, and laboratory technicians with scientists. There were possibly about 20 000 of the former and 2000 of the latter.

Subordinate medical services, too, have flourished: from 8200 in 1911 to 51 600 in 1951. They include physiotherapists, masseurs, opticians and similar crafts. The number of nurses has also increased substantially, especially in their male constituent:

	1911	*1951*	
	000s	*000s*	*% of 1911*
Males	1.5	29.0	1933
Females	94.3	237.4	252

The number of teachers has risen by only 22 per cent, no faster than the rise in the labour force. Here again there has been a disproportionate rise in the number of males. In 1911 there were 2.6 women to each male teacher; in 1951 only 1.6.

Over the forty years, the number of artists rose from 13 200 to 17 600, mostly an addition of men. But, sadly, the number of musicians fell, from 51 000 to 29 000, and the number of actors and entertainers from 19 000 to 15 000.

Employers, proprietors, managers, administrators

Those in Occupational Class 2 formed 10.14 per cent of all those occupied in 1911, and 10.5 per cent in 1951. This was because the fall in the proportion of employers and proprietors was compensated for by the rise in the proportion of managers and administrators. The distinction is partly one of law, for when a business is incorporated, the employers *ipso facto* become employees of the company. Class 2 does not include people in Class 1, for their profession is given precedence over their industrial status, and it includes only those proprietors for whose occupation the control of property is decisive.

The biggest group in Class 2A consists of employers and proprietors in the distributive trade, whose numbers rose from 495 000 in 1911 to 579 000 in 1931, and fell to 440 000 in 1951. Next come the farmers whose numbers rose and fell as follows:

	000s
1911	245
1921	302
1931	277
1951	302

In Class 2B, the number of managers and administrators rose steadily from 629 000 in 1911 to 1 246 000 in 1951. In 1911, there were 24 employees in Classes 3 to 7 for each manager; in 1951, there were 15.

Clerical workers

The rise in the number of clerks, as we have noted, exceeded that of any other class between 1911 and 1951. Strangely enough, the most rapid increase occurred between 1911 and 1921, with +47 per cent for the decade. Between 1921 and 1931 it was only +13 per cent, while over the next twenty years it averaged 28 per cent per decade. Over the two world war periods, the rate of increase of females greatly exceeded that of males. In 1931, males still constituted 56 per cent of the class; in 1951, only 41 per cent. By 1951, one woman in five of those gainfully employed was a clerk.

Foremen, supervisors, inspectors

As we have seen, this class increased from 1.29 per cent of the labour force in 1911 to 2.62 per cent in 1951. There was, in general, a fall in the number of employees per foreman or woman, for example from 29 to 14 in coalmining, 24 to 15 in chemicals and 54 to 12 in metal-making and metal-working. It was only in building and contracting that the number rose, from 13 to 16 (Routh, 1965, p. 28).

The development of mass production in the engineering industry has seen the emergence of a class of 'inspectors, viewers, testers', distinguished first for the electrical industry in 1921, but for engineering in general only in 1951. In that year they numbered 126 000.

Women have constituted a small but rising proportion of Class 4:

	%
1906	4.1
1921	6.6
1931	8.6
1951	13.3

Skilled manual workers

As we saw in Table 3.1, the number of workers in Class 5 hardly changed between 1911 and 1951, so that there was a fall in the relative size of the class, from 30.56 per cent in 1911 to 24.95 per cent in 1951. This was compounded from a *rise* of half a million men and a *fall* of half a million women.

By far the biggest group for men in 1911 consisted of skilled metal-makers and metal-workers, while that for women was textiles. But by 1951, those in the metal trades had increased by 63 per cent to just over two million, while the number of skilled women in textiles had been halved. The number of skilled women in the leather and clothing industries had also been drastically reduced (see Routh, 1965, p.129).

Semi-skilled manual workers

Table 3.1 shows a rise of 94 000 in Class 6. All but 6000 of these were women. But there were marked contrasts in the fortunes of the various industries from which their employment was derived. Semi-skilled employment in manufacturing increased from 1 030 000 in 1911 to 1 265 000 in 1951; other ranks in the armed services increased from 196 000 to 531 000. Other changes reveal some of the social history of these forty years:

		000s	
		1911	1951
Indoor domestic servants			
in private households	M	45	9
	F	1403	343
in hotels, lodging houses, etc.	M	13	62
	F	67	454
Total		1528	868
Agricultural labourers, foresters,			
fishermen	M	1188	707
	F	100	88
Shop assistants	M	588	459
	F	342	652
Catering and personal services	M	167	272
	F	308	388
Vehicle drivers			
Horse		404	15
Trams, trolley buses		17	13
Motor		50	547

Domestic servants had priced themselves out of the range of many private households at the same time that education and other areas of employment were presenting alternatives. Agriculture offered a similar reservoir from which male labour could be drawn. Just as women had become predominant in offices, they now became so in shops.

Unskilled manual workers

Workers in Class 7 increased from 1911 to 1931 and decreased from 1931 to 1951:

		000s		
	1911	*1921*	*1931*	*1951*
Men	1493	2280	2645	2158
Women	274	460	467	550
All	1767	2740	3115	2709

Labouring jobs, requiring strength without skill, are mainly performed by men; charing and office cleaning is mainly done by women and occupied more than two-fifths of the women in Class 7 in 1951. But women have been used to replace men in some unskilled occupations in time of war and, owing to the scarcity of male labour, they tended to remain there after 1945. There were 1000 women working as building labourers in 1951 and over 2000 as railway porters. Their numbers increased, too, in some manufacturing industries:

		000s	
		1931	*1951*
Chemical and allied trades	M	57.0	60.8
	F	9.5	12.7
Metal-working, engineering, electrical and allied trades	M	315.8	467.5
	F	32.8	61.2

4 1951–1981

4.1 CENSUS CHANGES

Those who believe in an innate tendency to social improvement might expect population censuses to get better and better as time goes by. This did indeed happen until 1951, though there were a few lapses along the way. In 1901, the authorities presented a single table aggregating the occupational data for the United Kingdom, while including separate columns for England and Wales, Scotland and Ireland. After that those who wished to combine the data for Great Britain or the United Kingdom had to do it for themselves. In 1931, tricks were played with the status categories, managers and employers being combined under the title 'managerial'. This was repeated in 1961, while in the semi-decennial census of 1966, employers and self-employed were combined as 'self-employed with and without employees'. Happily, in 1971 there was a return to the style of 1951, and occupational tables were published for the whole of Great Britain.

In 1951, 584 occupations had been distinguished, but in a curious fit of parsimony this was reduced to 201 in 1961. In 1971, this was extended to 223, and not until 1981 was there once more an approach to the expansive style of 1951, with a list of 549 units.

In the introduction to the occupation and industry tables for 1961 the General Register Office explained:

> Comparison of occupation figures for 1951 and 1961 is very difficult as the occupation classification has been completely revised. The occupations stated in a sub-sample of census forms from the 1961 Census have been coded according to both the *Classification of Occupations, 1960* and the Census 1951, *Classification of Occupations*. Due to the uncertain validity of this comparison it is not intended to publish the results of this exercise. However details can be made available if required. (General Register Office, 1965, p. iii)

From the sub-sample, two sets of tables were compiled, one showing occupations in 1951 and 1961 on the 1951 classification, the other doing the same on the 1960 classification. Illuminating though this may be, it is not possible to distinguish the self-employed and employers from each other or from employees, for the tables do not show industrial status, nor are data provided for Scotland.

4.2 MANUAL AND NON-MANUAL WORKERS

In October 1968, the Department of Employment introduced its 'New Earnings Survey'. Since April 1970, this has been held annually. It is a sample survey of employees in employment, showing their occupations and industries as well as their earnings. It does not include employers, the unemployed or the self-employed, but none the less it is a useful source of occupational data that can be used to amplify that given in the census. In the following chapter, we shall use it to gauge current trends.

Comparisons with 1961 are particularly difficult, though movements in particular occupations can be followed and certain broad measures applied. This has been done for 1961 by Bain and Price (1972) and Knight (1967). It is from the work of these scholars that the figures for 1961 are drawn in Table 4.1.

Table 4.1   Distribution of manual and non-manual workers, census years 1951–81

		Percentages			
		1951	*1961*	*1971*	*1981*
1	Professional	6.63	9.00	11.07	14.66
2	Employers, managers proprietors	10.50	10.10	12.43	13.98
3	Clerical	10.68	12.70	13.90	14.80
4–7	Foremen and manual workers	72.19	68.10	62.60	56.55
	All	100	100	100	100

In Chapter 3 I remarked on the persistent domination of the manual-working proletariat, but after 1951 the process of erosion is clearly marked. Between 1921 and 1951, Classes 5, 6 and 7, as a proportion of the labour force, lost 7.27 percentage points; between 1951 and 1981, they lost 17.24. At this rate, by 1991 they will have become a minority of the working population.

4.3   OCCUPATIONAL CLASSES 1951, 1971, 1981

Table 4.2 presents the data for the occupational classes in total and by sex. It is the lower professionals who lead the expansion. Their numbers nearly doubled in the thirty years preceding 1951, and multiplied by a factor of more than 2½ in the thirty years succeeding. The higher professions almost maintained their rate of expansion, and managers and administrators showed a moderate increase in theirs. Employers and proprietors doubled their rate of decline, from 10 per cent in the period 1911–51, to 20 per cent in the period 1951–81. The rise of clerical workers declined from a factor of 2.7 for the period 1911–51 to one of 1.6 for the subsequent thirty years, while the number of manual workers fell relatively and absolutely:

	1981 as % of 1951
1A Higher professions	227.6
1B Lower professions	258.4
2A Employers and proprietors	80.9
2B Managers and administrators	212.5
3 Clerical workers	156.4
4 Foremen, inspectors, supervisors	181.7
5 Skilled manual	79.6
6 Semi-skilled manual	86.2
7 Unskilled manual	91.8
All	112.8

In 1951, less than two in one hundred of the occupied population were in the higher professions; in 1981, the figure was just under four. In the lower professions there were less than five per hundred in 1951, in 1981 more than ten. Thus the labour force is being enriched. But what are we to make of the rise in the proportion of managers and foremen – just over eight per hundred in 1951 and nearly fifteen in 1981? This seems to be a great many people to employ in seeing that the rest of us do our work. And why should so many more be necessary now than thirty years ago? Of course, their task is not only to maintain discipline, but also (perhaps mainly?) to *organise*, a function that includes relieving those they supervise of unnecessary labour. This function is seen at its most specialised in the firms of management consultants who, because they are free of preconceptions and bureaucratic vested interests, are particularly good at

Table 4.2 Occupational classes by sex, 1951, 1971, 1981 (in thousands)

		1951			1971			1981		
		All	M	F	All	M	F	All	M	F
Professional										
1A Higher		434	399	36	824	774	50	988	885	103
	%	1.93	2.56	0.52	3.29	4.87	0.55	3.89	5.70	1.04
1B Lower		1059	492	567	1946	946	1000	2736	1187	1549
	%	4.70	3.16	8.18	7.78	5.95	10.94	10.77	7.64	15.68
2A Employers, etc.		1118	894	223	1056	805	251	904	675	229
	%	4.97	5.74	3.22	4.22	5.07	2.75	3.56	4.35	2.32
2B Managers, etc.		1246	1056	189	2054	1733	321	2648	2138	509
	%	5.53	6.78	2.73	8.21	10.91	3.51	10.42	13.77	5.15
3 Clerical		2404	990	1414	3479	1013	2466	3761	887	2874
	%	10.68	6.35	20.40	13.90	6.38	26.99	14.80	5.71	29.09
4 Foremen, etc.		590	511	79	968	801	168	1072	811	262
	%	2.62	3.28	1.14	3.87	5.04	1.84	4.22	5.22	2.65
Manual workers										
5 Skilled		5616	4733	884	5410	4647	763	4470	3959	511
	%	24.94	30.37	12.76	21.62	29.25	8.35	17.59	25.50	5.17
6 Semi-skilled		7098	4294	2805	6162	3285	2877	6121	3399	2722
	%	31.53	27.55	40.48	24.63	20.68	31.48	24.09	21.89	27.55
7 Unskilled		2949	2215	733	3125	1882	1243	2706	1586	1120
	%	13.10	14.21	10.58	12.49	11.85	13.60	10.65	10.21	11.34
All		22513	15584	6930	25021	15884	9138	25406	15527	9879
	%	100	100	100	100	100	100	100	100	100

increasing efficiency by improved organisation. The rise in the proportion of clerical workers is another rather alarming phenomenon, although, as we shall see in Chapter 5, this trend has now been weakened though not yet reversed.

Table 4.2 gives evidence of the continued subordination of women. At such time as they constitute half the occupants of Classes 1A, 2B and 4, they will have achieved equality. There is a long way to go, for in 1981 they formed only 10.4 per cent, 19.2 per cent and 24.4 per cent respectively of these three classes. At the same time, their range of occupational choice has expanded enormously, relieving them of the claustrophobia of those times when their choice was largely between textile mills or domestic service. They now dominate the clerical and lower professions. Their rate of increase in white-collar occupations greatly exceeds that of men, but, of course, in management and the higher professions is from a much lower base.

It has been possible to maintain consistency for the first four classes, with their subdivisions, from 1911 to 1981. Methods were described in Routh (1965 and 1980), but changes in classification and the elimination of detail have prevented the same consistency for Classes 5, 6 and 7. Table 3.1, for the years 1911 to 1951, used the classification and social class allocation of 1951, with which previous censuses were brought into line. Difficulties, however, have accumulated, for which reason it was decided for the period now dealt with to base comparisons on the usages of 1981.

This does not affect Classes 1 to 4, but entails some changes in Classes 5, 6 and 7. In Table 3.1, kitchen hands were allocated to Occupational Class 6, along with domestic servants. Domestic servants are rightly graded as semi-skilled and kitchen hands as unskilled, but because in earlier years they were not distinguished, the latter were also included in Class 6. In 1951, 1961 and 1971, kitchen hands were given an entry of their own, but in the census of 1981 they were included with kitchen porters. For comparisons post-1951, it is advisable to allocate them to Occupational Class 7.

Another amalgamation of 1981 has necessitated the transfer of window cleaners and chimney sweeps from the semi-skilled to the unskilled group, for they have been included with cleaners and road sweepers. In Table 4.2 they have accordingly been transferred to Class 7 for 1951 and 1971. Coalminers, too, were subjected to amalgamation in 1981. The census of 1951 distinguished machine cutters, other face workers, and seven other mining occupations, while that of 1981 specifies only two: face-trained coalmining workers and coalmining labourers. Despite the term 'labourer', they are graded as semi-skilled in the census social class and socio-economic group classification, and so have been placed in Occupational Class 6 in Table 4.2.

There is, however, one group of workers for whom the amalgamation of 1981 has been rejected: warehousemen, storemen and assistant storemen. As with most linked occupations, there is not a sharp division between them, but the scale and complexity of their duties does permit them to be distinguished in systems of job classification and evaluation. They were shown separately in the census of 1951, but pooled in 1961 and subsequent years. Their numbers are considerable (333 000 in 1981), so it is worth separating them; I have done this for 1971 and 1981 in the same proportions as those shown in the census for 1951:

	Percentages	
	Males	*Females*
Warehousemen	36.8	7.8
Storekeepers	52.3	13.4
Assistants	10.8	78.8
All	100	1100

I hope that in 1991 the authorities may be persuaded to restore the usage of 1951, so that the need for this device is eliminated.

All this has resulted in some differences in Classes 5, 6 and 7 with respect to 1951 as between Table 3.1 and Table 4.2:

	Allocations to Classes 5, 6 and 7	
	for 1951 (000s)	
Manual workers	Table 3.1	Table 4.2
5 Skilled	5616	5616
6 Semi-skilled	7338	7098
7 Unskilled	2709	2949

We may construct a continuous index of the rise or decline of these groups from 1911 to 1981 and beyond, using 1951 as a link in the series. In future, it will be difficult for the Office of Population Censuses and Surveys to introduce the sort of arbitrary changes with which we have been afflicted in the past, for they have now joined the Department of Employment in employing the *Classification of Occupations and Directory of Occupational Titles* (CODOT), with its abstract of 400 *Key Occupations for Statistical Purposes* (KOS) (published in three volumes by the Department of Employment, HMSO, 1972).

4.4 DISTRIBUTION BY STATUS, 1981

1981 is used as a pivotal year, from which we look back at 1951, and from which enterprising scholars, whose interest has been aroused, may assess 1991 and even (who knows?) 2081. To facilitate such comparisons, Table 4.3 shows the occupational classes by industrial status and sex. I remind you that all professional workers are placed in Occupational Class 1, even though their status is that of employer, manager or foreman; all other employers are allocated to Class 2A, all other managers and administrators to Class 2B, all other foremen to Class 4.

There still exist a great many unincorporated businesses – that is, businesses where the employer is a real and not only a legal person. Thus in 1981, more than 700 000 economically active people were employers. Another 1.2 million were self-employed (or working on their own account). Their numbers are no doubt increasing as people struggle to escape from the pain of unemployment. Between 1951 and 1981, the number of employers rose faster than the occupied population, the number of self-employed slower.

4.5 CHANGES WITHIN CLASSES

We have seen that the numbers in Class 1A more than doubled between 1951 and 1981. But the rate of increase slackened considerably in the decade 1971–81 – just under 2 per cent per year, compared with a little over 3¼ per cent per year for the previous twenty years. The spectacular rise in the number of engineers, architects and surveyors had come to an end. Between 1951 and 1971, their numbers had tripled, but then increased by less than 14 per cent between 1971 and 1981. Amongst the other higher professions, expansion continued, with only the clergy registering a decline.

Class 1B, the lower professionals, expanded by 83.8 per cent between 1951 and 1971, and by 40.6 per cent 1971 and 1981. The annual compound rate, 3.1 per cent in the first twenty years, increased to 3.4 per cent in the last ten, thus providing 790 000 additional jobs in the decade to 1981.

Table 4.3 Occupational class and industrial status by sex, 1981 (in thousands)

	Employers	Own account	Managers	Foremen	Other employees	Unemployed	All
Men							
1 Professional							
A Higher	89.0	52.7	33.7	—	686.3	23.5	885.2
B Lower	21.8	63.5	117.6	25.1	913.4	46.0	1187.4
2 Managerial							
A Employers, proprietors	443.1	231.9	—	—	—	—	675.0
B Managers, administrators	—	61.9	1652.0	—	332.3	102.1	2138.3
3 Clerical	—	7.8	—	100.8	733.5	45.1	887.2
4 Foremen, inspectors	—	0.6	—	604.8	150.9	54.4	810.6
Manual workers							
5 Skilled	—	361.0	—	—	3176.6	421.0	3958.6
6 Semi-skilled	—	150.7	—	—	2852.6	395.5	3398.9
7 Unskilled	—	47.0	—	—	864.1	674.5	1585.6
All	553.9	977.0	1803.3	730.7	9699.7	1762.0	15526.7

43

Women

1 Professional							
A Higher	5.9	10.5	4.2	—	79.3	3.3	103.2
B Lower	11.5	36.3	73.5	73.4	1309.2	45.0	1548.9
2 Managerial							
A Employers, proprietors	131.1	98.1	—	—	—	—	229.1
B Managers, administrators	—	28.3	413.3	—	47.8	19.9	509.3
3 Clerical	—	23.7	—	113.6	2632.4	104.1	2873.8
4 Foremen, inspectors	—	0.2	—	135.6	110.1	15.8	261.7
Manual workers							
5 Skilled	—	10.0	—	—	463.9	37.0	510.9
6 Semi-skilled	—	20.6	—	—	2535.9	165.4	2721.9
7 Unskilled	—	7.2	—	—	775.8	337.1	1120.1
All	148.5	235.0	491.1	322.6	7954.4	727.4	9878.9

About half the members of the class are teachers or nurses, whose increase was below the average (13 and 37 per cent respectively), so that the major increases were spread over a number of smaller groups. These included:

		1981 as % of 1971
Draughtsmen and -women		152
Welfare workers	M	278
	F	295
Others in medicine	M	137
(other than those in Class 1A)	F	350

Employers and proprietors continued on the downward path, with a decline of 7½ per cent in the former and 24 per cent in the latter, while managers and administrators remained on the ascendant. Between 1951 and 1971 their growth was 2½ per cent compound per year, and in the ensuing decade only slightly less. This was achieved by an annual growth of 2.1 per cent for men and 4.7 per cent for women. But in 1981 there were more than two million men in the class, and only half a million women. If their respective rates of increase persist, women will overtake men about the middle of the year 2059. But since there would then have to be more managers and administrators than people for them to manage and administrate, women in the class will have to raise their rate of increase drastically if they are ever to achieve equality with men.

You may see from Table 4.2 that the advance of clerical workers (Class 3) continued in the decade to 1981. Their rate remained in excess of that of the total occupied, so that in 1971 they formed 13.9 per cent of the total, and in 1981 had advanced to 14.8 per cent. Factory workers have declined, while their output has risen, because of advances in mechanisation and organisation, but the expectations of those who predicted the same fate for office workers have been disappointed. However, there are two effects to be noted: the *rate* of increase has declined from 45 per cent between 1951 and 1971, and 8 per cent between 1971 to 1981 (from 1.9 per cent per year to 0.8 per cent), while the number of male clerical workers has actually fallen:

	000s	
	1971	1981
Males	1013	887
Females	2466	2873

It may be that the women had also passed their peak and, by 1981, were already in decline. This is something we shall explore in the next chapter.

Table 4.2 shows an increase of 100 000 in the number of foremen, inspectors and supervisors between 1971 and 1981, at a time when the total number of manual workers fell by a million. After the Second World War great stress was laid on the importance of supervision and a campaign was promoted for 'Training Within Industry for Supervisors' (TWI). The returns for good supervision were demonstrated and, in response, the ratio of supervisors to workers was increased. A comparison of the occupation tables of 1971 and 1981 suggests that this process may have run its course in metal-making and metal-working (with seven process workers per foreman, supervisor or inspector in each year) and building and contracting, with five in 1971 and six in 1981). But in chemicals there was a further reduction from six to four workers per supervisor, and in textiles from thirteen to eight. Of course, machines have to be supervised as well as people, and as the former advance, the latter recede. Women constitute an increasing proportion of the class: there were 827 men to 173 women in 1971, and 756 to 244 in 1981.

In 1981 nearly half the skilled workers (Class 5) were employed in the metal-making and metal-using trades. Of these, half again were in the following occupations:

	000s
Metal-working production fitters and fitter machinists	512
Production fitters (electrical, electronic), electricity power plant operators, switchboard attendants	317
Welders	149
Sheet-metal workers, platers, shipwrights, riveters, etc.	130
	1108

Only 2¼ per cent of these were women.

Changes in the major groups are shown in Table 4.4. For most of them a combination of circumstances has resulted in a general decline: deskilling of the production process as automation displaces people, a drift from manufacturing to services (especially financial services) and the onset of depression. There may have been a slight rise in the building group between 1971 and 1981 (see the notes to

Table 4.4), but more of them were unemployed: less than 40 000 in 1971, and 62 000 in 1981.

Table 4.4   Skilled manual workers: major constituents of Class 5, employees (including those unemployed) and self-employed, 1951–81 (in thousands)

	1951	1971	1981
Coal hewers and getters	226	96	66
Metal-makers and metal-workers	2096	2356	2114
Textiles	445	168	107
Leather and textile goods	379	(187)	54
Paper and printing	279	292	169
Building, civil engineering, decorating	582	(520)	526
Hairdressers, barbers	83	129	92
Workers in wood, cane and cork	461	390	415

Notes: The 1971 classification does not permit a satisfactory allocation between skilled and semi-skilled clothing workers. In 1961 and 1971 a substantial number of construction workers were lumped together as 'Construction workers n.e.c.' (= not elsewhere classified). These have been divided by skill according to the Census Department's reconciliation of the 1951 and 1961 occupational tables for England and Wales, the results of which were not published but are available on request.

In 1951, the 'golden age' of censuses, the Registrar General identified twelve classes of mineworker: three skilled and nine semi-skilled. These were reduced in the not-so-good days of 1961 to six, in the worse days of 1971 to four with no distinction by skill, and in 1981 to two: face-trained coalmining workers and, amongst 'labourers and unskilled workers n.e.c.', 60 460 men and 280 women in coal-mines.

Table 4.5 identifies twelve occupations that, between them, accounted for 84 per cent of Class 6 (semi-skilled manual workers) in 1951. In their jobs, manual dexterity and physical exertion are combined with a need to exercise the mind, but the required skills can be learnt within a matter of weeks.

The biggest group consisted of those engaged in manufacturing industry. They are process workers (those directly engaged in making the relevant product) or craftsmen's mates. The process workers, in the main, work as machine minders or machine tool operators, or as assemblers. They are people who have been particularly hit by the advent of robots and automation, yet employment between 1951 and 1971 fell by only 9 per cent, and between 1971 and 1981 by less than 3

Table 4.5   Semi-skilled manual workers: major constituents of Class 6, employees (including those unemployed) and self-employed, 1951–81 (in thousands)

	1951	1971	1981
Manufacturing	1606	1459	1419
Distributive trades	1111	984	988
Drivers of road vehicles	575	710	725
Packers and storekeepers	386	(488)	(405)
Waiters, bar staff, counter hands and assistants	173	404	467
Farm workers, foresters, fishermen	795	410	337
NCOs and other ranks, armed forces	531	218	231
Indoor private domestic servants	352	198	91
Postmen, mailsorters	99	126	125
Telephone operators	87	106	87
Launderers, dry cleaners, pressers	130	82	55
Bus and tram conductors	97	58	17

Note: in 1971 and 1981, warehousemen, storekeepers and their assistants were not distinguished from one another. They are here divided in the proportions obtaining in 1951.

per cent. It was sustained in part by the rapid expansion in the production of electrical and electronic goods.

Shop assistants, too, fell in number by only 11 per cent between 1951 and 1971, and showed a fractional percentage increase in the next ten years. Between 1951 and 1971 the number of men was halved, while that of women rose by 18 per cent, but after that the proportions of the sexes held steady. Farm labourers, foresters and fishermen continued their decline, and so did indoor private domestic servants, and launderers and dry cleaners. Bus and tram conductors are a vanishing race, while packers and storekeepers first rose in numbers and then declined. The decline was divided almost equally between the packers, bottlers, canners and fillers on the one hand, and storekeepers on the other.

The unskilled workers (Occupational Class 7) are *ipso facto* less differentiated than those whose jobs require perceptible skill. This is not to say that the jobs in which they are employed do not present contrasts to one another: some require strength and endurance, others idleness and boredom. The unskilled generally constitute about half of the unemployed, though only one-eighth or ninth of the employed:

Unskilled workers, employed and unemployed (000s)			
	1951	1971	1981
Males in employment	2115	1550	909
unemployed	100	332	677
Females in employment	718	967	785
unemployed	15	276	335

I have already mentioned the difficulties caused by the drastic reduction of occupations distinguished in the tables of 1961 and 1971, the merging of sub-orders with different levels of skill and the immoderate use of the portmanteau term 'n.e.c.' (not elsewhere classified). For example, in 1971, out of 816 940 construction workers (including building and contracting labourers) 252 840 were designated as 'not elsewhere classified'. In the tables shown above I have contrived to separate them by following the divisions shown in the Registrar General's sample reclassification of the 1961 occupational tables for England and Wales in terms of the categories of 1951. Unfortunately this removes the phenomenon that we specially wish to measure: the *change* in the proportions between censuses.

In 1981, the census authorities (by that time the Office of Population Censuses and Surveys, with the Registrar General, Scotland), conforming with the official *Classification of Occupations and Directory of Occupational Titles* (CODOT), re-expanded their list of occupations, thus facilitating comparisons with 1951. One important deficiency, on the other hand, has become more serious: the numbers of those whose occupations are listed as 'inadequately described and not stated'. A few of these are employers, managers or foremen, but the great majority are unemployed.

The census calls for 'full and precise details of the occupation', and the official enumerators are supposed to ensure that the forms are properly completed, but despite this the numbers of those inadequately described have multiplied from 80 000 in 1951 to 645 000 in 1971 to more than 950 000 in 1981. This has been associated with the great rise in unemployment that has marked this period:

	Registered unemployed, April each year (000s)
1951	253
1971	727
1981	2279

The probability is that most of those who have not stated their occupation have not done so, despite the enumerators' queries, because they have no occupation to state, or because they have had various jobs to none of which they feel attached. In these circumstances it seems appropriate to include them with the unskilled. The major constituents of this class are shown in Table 4.6.

Table 4.6   Unskilled manual workers: major constituents of Class 7, employees (including those unemployed) and self-employed, 1951–81 (in thousands)

	1951		1971		1981	
	M	F	M	F	M	F
Labourers and other unskilled workers in building and civil engineering	492	1	386	2	208	1
in other industrial and commercial undertakings	1063	211	803	134	450	48
Warehouse and storekeepers' assistants	52	30	39	60	31	37
Kitchen hands	20	182	19	103	20[a]	101[a]
Charwomen, office cleaners	14	238	66	423	122[b]	505[b]
Chimney sweeps, window cleaners	38	1				
Dock labourers, stevedores	81	—	38	—	25	—
Costermongers and other hawkers[c]	34	5	52	14	18	7
Lorry drivers' mates, vanguards	36	2	20	—	11	—
Messengers, porters, lift attendants, doorkeepers	192	7	59	6	132	11
Boiler firemen and stokers	80	—	36	—	18[d]	—
Inadequately described	55	26	271	374	544	409

[a] inc. kitchen porters
[b] inc. road sweepers
[c] inc. newspaper sellers, scrapdealers, rag and bone sorters
[d] boiler operators

5 Retrospect

5.1 HISTORY UNFOLDING

In the winter of 1801 a small army went out into the English and Welsh countryside to count the inhabitants. The Scots, very sensibly, postponed their count until the following summer. For each parish, an enumerator was designated: in England and Wales the local rector, vicar, curate or minister; in Scotland, the schoolmaster. Their task was to determine the number of males and females in the parish; the number of persons chiefly employed in agriculture; the number employed in trade, manufactures or handicraft; the number of soldiers, sailors and merchant seamen; and of convicts awaiting transportation on board the hulks. The results are shown in Table 5.1.

The population, nearly eleven million, was one-fifth of that of today, and was quite small even for those days. But though France and Germany were more than twice as populous, no other country had a capital as big as London with its one million inhabitants. Paris was half that size, Vienna a quarter, Berlin one-sixth (Armengaud, 1970, p. 19). But the kingdom had very little else to show – there were only seven towns with populations of more than fifty thousand, namely:

	000s
Edinburgh	83
Liverpool	82
Glasgow	77
Manchester	75
Birmingham	71
Bristol	61
Leeds	53

(Mitchell and Deane, 1962, p. 24)

Six generations ago, in the early 1800s, three-quarters of our great-great-great-grandfathers and -mothers lived in villages or the countryside, ruled by a political system that had long since degenerated into an oligarchy in which parliamentary seats could be bought or sold. In 1799 a law had been enacted making it illegal for any

Table 5.1 The total and occupied populations of England, Wales and Scotland, 1801 or 1802

	Males	Females	All	Agriculture	Occupations Trade manufactures handicrafts	Others
England	3987935	4343499	8331434	1524227	1789531	4606530
Wales	257178	284368	541546	189062	53822	266573
Scotland	734581	864487	1599068	365516	293373	833914
Army	198351					198351
Navy	126279					126279
Seamen	144558					144558
In the hulks[a]	1410					1410
Total	5450292	5492354	10942646	2078805	2136726	6177615

[a]Convicts awaiting transportation.

Source: Census Reports 1801, Abstract of the Answers and Returns (reprinted London: Frank Cass, 1968).

workman to combine with any other workman to get higher pay or shorter hours, or to attend a meeting aimed at so doing.

Many of those counted in the census of 1801, their children and their children's children, were to endure great suffering through the ignorance, indifference and greed of those who ruled their lives. But there were landmarks of progress. The 'rotten boroughs' were abolished by the Reform Act of 1832, the Combination Acts were repealed in 1824, and slowly and painfully, under pressure of great campaigns, legislation was passed to limit the hours of women and children in mines and factories, and to protect trade unions from actions under civil and criminal law.

Hardship and poverty resulted from low wages, scarcity and irregularity of employment, unhealthy conditions in housing, mines and factories, and lack of time for rest and leisure. Real wages rose erratically, but it was not until the middle of the nineteenth century that a process of slow but general amelioration set in. Robert Owen (1771–1858) lived through the Industrial Revolution and helped to set in train this process of amelioration, by the example of his textile factory at New Lanark and his tireless promotion of trade unions and factory legislation. He observed in 1815:

Those who were engaged in the trade, manufactures, and commerce of this country thirty or forty years ago formed but a very insignificant portion of the knowledge, wealth, influence, or population of the Empire.

Prior to that period, Britain was essentially agricultural. But from that time to the present, the home and foreign trade have increased in a manner so rapid and extraordinary as to have raised commerce to an importance, which it never previously attained in any country possessing so much political power and influence...

These important results, however, great as they really are, have not been obtained without accompanying evils of such a magnitude as to raise a doubt whether the latter do not preponderate over the former...

Not more than thirty years since, the poorest parents thought the age of fourteen sufficiently early for their children to commence regular labour... It should be remembered also that twelve hours per day, including the time for regular rest and meals, were then thought sufficient to extract all the working strength of the most robust adult; when it may be remarked local holidays were much more frequent than at present in most parts of the kingdom.

At this period, too, they were generally trained by the example of some landed proprietor, and in such habits as created a mutual interest between the parties, by which means even the lowest peasant was considered as belonging to, and forming somewhat of a member of, a respectable family...

Contrast this state of matters with that of the lower orders of the present day... In the manufacturing districts it is common for parents to send their children of both sexes at seven or eight years of age, in winter as well as summer, at six o'clock in the morning, sometimes of course in the dark, and occasionally amidst frost and snow, to enter the manufactories, which are often heated to a high temperature, and contain an atmosphere far from being the most favourable to human life, and in which all those employed in them very frequently continue until twelve o'clock at noon, when an hour is allowed for dinner, after which they return to remain, in a majority of cases, till eight o'clock at night.

The children now find they must labour incessantly for their bare subsistence: they have not been used to innocent, healthy and rational amusements... They know not what relaxation means, except by the actual cessation from labour... The employer regards the employed as mere instruments of gain, while these acquire a gross ferocity of character, which, if legislative measures shall not be judiciously devised to prevent its increase, and ameliorate the condition of this class, will sooner or later plunge the country into a formidable and perhaps inextricable state of danger.

(quoted in Cole and Filson, 1951, pp. 8–12)

Conditions were to get worse under the onslaught of industrialisation, so that in 1842 the Commissioners on the Employment of Children shocked respectable middle-class people by their report:

Helen Reid, sixteen years old, coal-bearer: 'I have wrought five years in the mines in this part; my employment is carrying coal. Am frequently worked from four in the morning until six at night. I work night-work week about. I then go down at two in the day, and come up at four and six in the morning. I can carry near two cwt on my back. I do not like the work. Two years since the pit closed upon 13 of us, and we were two days without food or light; nearly one day we were up to our chins in water. At last we got to an old shaft, to which we picked our way, and were heard by people watching above. Two months ago I was filling the tubs at the pit bottom, when the gig clicked too early, and the hook caught me by my pit-clothes – the people did not hear my shrieks – my hand had fast grappled the chain, and the great height of the shaft caused me to lose my courage, and I swooned. The banksman could scarcely remove my hand – the deadly grasp saved my life'.

A sub-commissioner summed up his observations thus:

Now, when the nature of this horrible labour is taken into consideration, its extreme severity, its regular duration of from 12 to 14 hours daily, the damp, heated, and unwholesome atmosphere of a coal-mine, and the tender age and sex of the workers – a picture is presented of deadly physical oppression and systematic slavery, of which I conscientiously believe no one unacquainted with such facts would credit the existence in the British dominions. (Children's Employment Commission, 1842, pp. 28 and 29; J. L. and Barbara Hammond, 1949, review this and other evidence)

For extreme ills, the victims sought extreme solutions. King Ludd, Captain Swing, the Grand National Consolidated Trades Union, Chartism, the National Reform Union, the Sheffield Outrages, the New Model Trade Unions, the International Working Men's Association: there was no end of subversive movements to keep on edge the nerves of well-to-do people who asked nothing but the right to enjoy the fruits of other people's labour. But the ruling classes yielded, sometimes it seemed just in time, so that Britain remained immune to the revolutions that were enforcing change on the countries of Continental Europe.

In 1819, the Factory Act prohibited employment in the textile industry of children under the age of 9, and limited the working hours of persons under 16 to twelve hours per day, such hours to be between 5 am and 9 pm. In 1834, an Act prohibited boys of under 10 being apprenticed to a chimney sweep. From the middle of the century, successful unions of skilled workers emerged that won statutory protection in the 1870s. The match girls in 1888 and the dockers in 1889 demonstrated that the unskilled, too, could organise, or be organised, and assert themselves.

The industrial system that was emerging was highly unstable, with its alternating phases of prosperity and boom, slump and depression (there were fourteen recessions of various severity between 1803 and

Table 5.2   Wage rates and the cost of living,
1801–1981 (1801 = 100)

	Wage rates	Cost of living
1801	100	100
1811	127	92
1821	112	68
1831	104	72
1841	103	72
1851	107	54
1861	114	74
1871	131	75
1881	135	69
1891	145	57
1901	157	56
1911	154	56
1921	467	127
1931	309	85
1941	401	117
1951	660	176
1961	1082	248
1971	1924	391
1981	8374	1289

Sources: Wage rates, G. H. Wood (1899); A. L.
Bowley (1937), p. 6; Routh (1980), pp. 134–5.
Cost of living, Burnett (1969), pp. 199 and 307;
Employment Gazette, various issues.

1913), but they occurred on a rising trend (see Beveridge, 1960, p. 281). This may have been one reason why the revolution predicted by some failed to occur; another may have been the upward mobility of labour that was a characteristic of economic development, and that we shall shortly proceed to assess.

Table 5.2 gives a very rough measure of the amelioration of poverty over the 180 years to 1981. It is very rough because, as Adam Smith warned, 'The price of labour … cannot be ascertained very accurately anywhere, different prices being often paid at the same place and for the same sort of labour, not only according to the different abilities of the workmen, but according to the easiness or hardness of the masters' (Smith, 1776, p. 95). What G. H. Wood (1899), A. L. Bowley (1937) and the other statistical pioneers did was to put together what data they could find and, on that basis, construct indexes purporting to measure changes over time.

So the measures of Table 5.2 suggest that between 1801 and 1851, real wages more or less doubled. In 1851, money rates were not much different from their level of 1801, but prices had fallen by 50 per cent. Between 1851 and 1901, by contrast, money wages rose by 50 per cent while prices, having risen by nearly 40 per cent, returned to their former level. Over the century, then, real wages rose from 100 to 157/56 × 100 = 280. Then between 1901 and 1981, money wage rates went up by a factor of 53. With 1901 = 100, in 1981 they were 5333. In the same period, prices rose by a factor of 23, or in index form, with 1901 = 100, to 2302. So real wages had increased by 5333/2302, a factor of 2.3. The increase between 1801 and 1981 was thus 2.8 × 2.3 = 6.4.

5.2   THE GROWTH OF POPULATION

In his *Essay on Population*, Malthus assumed that population would grow as fast as its food supply allowed it to. Actually, as people become richer they also become meaner, or at least more prudent, marry later and voluntarily reduce the size of their families. Thus the Council on Environmental Quality (1982, p. 9) shows the populations of Pakistan and Nigeria increasing at 3 per cent per year, the average for less developed regions 2.1 per cent, and that for Western Europe 0.4 per cent. In their projection of the population of the United Kingdom from 1981 to 1991, the Office of Population Censuses and Surveys postulates a rate of increase of 0.19 per cent per year (Central Statistical Office, *Social Trends 1980*, p. 66). In the first four decades of the nineteenth century, by contrast, the annual increase in population ranged between nearly 1.4 and 1.7 per cent, so that numbers almost doubled between 1801 and 1851. The factors of growth over fifty-year periods were:

1801–1851	1.98
1851–1901	1.77
1901–1951	1.32

These population movements were common to European countries. How are they to be explained?

It would seem that somewhere between 1750 and 1800 the mortality rate began that process of decline which, with a few breaks, has continued until today. As one would expect, the decline began in the 'crisis death-rate'; i.e. the death-rate caused by famines, epidemics and wars. It was followed by a decline in the ordinary death-rate. This decline was a turning point in the history of European demography. To begin with, agricultural productivity was greatly increased due to improved farming methods, and quite particularly to the introduction of artificial manures, of new methods of crop rotation, and improvements in livestock resulting from planned in-breeding and cross-fertilisation. Large fluctuations from one harvest to the next were reduced, and with the exception of Ireland (1845–50), famine disappeared from Western Europe. (Armengaud, 1970, pp. 26–6)

There were great advances in medicine and public hygiene that manifested themselves particularly in the containment of epidemics and the decline in infant mortality.

It may be that the fall of the death rate itself contributed to a fall in the birth rate. Certainly, the development and popularisation of contraception made possible more effective family planning. These effects are associated with advances in wealth and education, both over time and in cross-sections of a society at any specified time. Of families registering legitimate births in 1977, the percentages that already had three or more children were as follows:

Father's occupational class	*% with 3 or more previous children*
Professional	3
Intermediate	5
Skilled non-manual	7
Skilled manual	10
Semi-skilled	14
Unskilled	5
All classes	7

(Central Statistical Office, *Social Trends 1980*, p. 88)

The inverse correlation between income and family size need not mean that children are a deterrent to the growth of national product. Francis Bacon wisely remarked, 'He that hath wife and children hath given hostages to fortune; for they are impediments to great enterprises, either of virtue or mischief'. But though they are impediments to great enterprises, they are incentives to small ones.

Directly, it is a question of what resources a household demands, and how they shall be deployed: in poor countries additional children may increase the under-nourishment of all; in rich ones they occasion increased expenditure on education and maternal and child-care, and less on beer, cars, videos and the other play-things of affluent man.

Children are paid for at the expense of parental leisure and, in due course, provide the additional labour with which economic growth is associated. In this respect they have acted as catalysts rather than impediments to growth. Of course, this is not how Malthus saw it, nor the imperialists of nineteenth-century Britain. By 1878 Cecil Rhodes had formed the idea 'of doing a great work for the over-crowded British public at home, by opening up fresh markets for their manufactures. . . He dwelt repeatedly on the fact that their great want was new territory fit for the overflow population to settle in permanently' (Jameson, 1897, p. 392). In 1895, Rhodes told William Stead: 'I was in the East End of London yesterday and attended a meeting of the unemployed. I listened to the wild speeches, which were just a cry for "bread! bread!", and on my way home I pondered the scene and I became more than ever convinced of the importance of imperialism' (quoted in Lenin, 1978, p. 75).

Paradoxically, after 1911 the rate of population growth was dramatically reduced, Britain lost its position as the world's leading industrial nation, and an almost endless series of economic crises began. All the same, in 1981, it supported a population nearly 70 per cent greater than in 1891 on a real wage-income more than 2½ times as high (Table 5.2, p. 55).

5.3   AGRICULTURE AND GROWTH

The distribution of workers between industries gives a measure of the stage a country has reached on its growth path: torpid, awakening, youth, maturity, arthritic old age. The clearest index is perhaps that of the decline in the numbers and proportion employed in agriculture. In Table 1.4 (p. 11), Booth shows the population of England and Wales in each census year and the numbers supported by agriculture (not in the sense of eating its products, but of living on the income derived from agricultural pursuits). The turning point comes in about 1851, after which the numbers employed and the proportion of the labour force so employed began their descent.

Booth gives his estimate of the numbers included in households

Table 5.3   Total population, numbers and percentage economically active, and percentage employed in agriculture, 1801–1981 (in thousands)

Year	Population Nos	Increase %	Economically active		
			Nos	%	of whom % agriculture
1801	10501	—	4800[a]	46	40
1811	11970	14	5500[a]	46	35[b]
1821	14092	18	6200[a]	44	33[b]
1831	16261	15	7200[a]	44	28[b]
1841	18534	14	8400	45	22
1851	20817	12	9377	45	22
1861	23128	11	10520	45	18
1871	26072	13	11870	46	15
1881	29710	14	12739	43	13
1891	33029	11	14499	44	10
1901	37000	12	16299	44	8.6
1911	40831	10	18385	45	8.2
1921	42769	5	19355	45	7.4
1931	44795	5	21055	47	6.4
1941	46908	5	21332	45	4.6
1951	48854	4	22610	46	5.4
1961	51284	5	23010	45	4.0
1971	53979	5	25021	46	2.9
1981	54285	0.6	25406	47	1.4

[a]Estimates from Deane and Cole (1969), p. 143. They warn: 'these figures must be used cautiously'.
[b]Percentage of *families* dependent on agriculture.

Sources: total population 1801–1951, Mitchell and Deane (1962) pp. 6–7; 1941: Feinstein (1976), p. T121. Economically active, 1941: Department of Employment, *Historical Statistics* (1971), p. 218.

whose principal income is derived from agriculture. Table 5.3, in its end column, shows the numbers employed in agriculture as a percentage of the labour force. Numbers in agriculture rise to their peak in 1851, but not as fast as the increase in the labour force, so that their relative decline is manifested from the beginning of the nineteenth century. In 1801, about 40 per cent of the economically active population worked in agriculture, in 1841 only 22 per cent. There is then a standstill in proportion, due, Booth suggests, to the influx of 400 000 people from Ireland (refugees from the potato famine), after which the decline continues, with a temporary switch between 1941 and 1951.

We have 2 136 000 employed in agriculture in Great Britain in 1801, a fall to 1 515 000 in 1841, a rise to 2 017 000 in 1851, until in 1981 numbers were down to 365 000. But while numbers and proportions declined, output held steady or expanded, which gives a measure of the advance in technology. Advances of knowledge have gone along with advances in mechanisation, chemistry and biology.

Between 1801 and 1861, Paul Rousseaux has the real product of agriculture, forestry and fishing growing at an annual compound rate of between 1.2 and 1.8 per cent (Deane and Cole, 1969, p. 170). Between 1855 and 1920, C. H. Feinstein's index of output for the same sector shows no upward trend. For the ten years 1855 to 1864, the index stood at an average of 99.8; for the ten years 1904 to 1913, the average was 101.0 (Feinstein, 1976, pp. 118–19).

The index produced by the London and Cambridge Economic Service (1958 = 100) shows an average of 34.4 for the fifteen years 1900 to 1914, 63.7 for the 1920s, and 71.0 for the years 1930 to 1938. During the war, agricultural production became part of the fight for survival, and after the war, for national solvency. The index rose from 78 in 1946 to 119 in 1963 (London and Cambridge Economic Service, n.d., p. 5).

Between 1801 and 1851, output doubled, while the labour force was reduced from 2 136 000 to 2 017 000. Between 1851 and 1981, output rose by a factor of 2¾, while the labour force declined by 82 per cent, from 2 017 000 to 365 010.

Table 5.4   Index of production for agriculture, forestry and fishing, 1801–1981

1801	100	1901	219
1811	113	1911	226
1821	127	1921	208
1831	147	1931	226
1841	176	1941	—
1851	200	1951	313
1861	215	1961	389
1871	228	1971	514
1881	230	1981	666
1891	243		

5.4   TEXTILES, ENGINEERING, RAILWAYS, COAL

In 1811, 1821 and 1831, as Booth explained, the census authorities held the idea that what they ought to measure was not the industrial distribution of working individuals, but the industrial dependence of families. They distinguished three groups: those dependent for their income on (1) agriculture, (2) trade, manufacturing or handicrafts, and (3) everything else.

Deane and Cole (1969, p. 142) essay to allocate economically active individuals among five productive sectors – a heroic contribution, as the Deputy Governor of the Bank of England once remarked about the work of a colleague of mine, from the bricks-without-straw department. The trouble is that in the present context these techniques of extra- or interpolation filter out the very effects we wish to measure.

So for the years after 1801 and before 1841 we must turn to other evidence to get a view of what was going on in transport, coal and manufacture. The Bridgewater canal was completed in 1758. McAdam began his experiments in road-building before the end of the eighteenth century, at which time, too, Metcalfe and Telford began working their wonders. The Liverpool–Manchester railway was opened in 1830.

James Watt had begun the manufacture of stationary steam-engines in 1774. They were used first in coal-mines, but in 1785 one was introduced into a cotton-spinning factory (Gibbins, 1903, p. 22). Spinning had been mechanised before the end of the eighteenth century, but though Cartwright had patented the power loom in 1785, it was not commercially applied until the first quarter of the following century (Gibbins, pp. 19–20). Innovation was restrained by the violence with which it was resisted by those whose jobs it endangered. King Ludd and Captain Swing had many variations.

Thus mechanised, the textile industry was about to conquer the world, destroying the spinners and weavers of India and other countries as well as the handloom operators at home. The hand weavers took a long time to go. G. H. Wood estimated that in the cotton industry in 1806 there were two of them for each factory worker, and that it was not until 1833–4 that their numbers were at par. By that year the total employed had risen by a factor of nearly 2½, while the consumption of raw cotton had increased fivefold. Then the number of handloom weavers began to fall from its peak of

240000 until, by 1860, it was down to 10000 (Mitchell and Deane, 1962, pp. 187 and 179).

As a measure of the growth of the engineering and metal-making industries, we may take as proxy the production of pig iron:

	000 tons	*Av. annual % increase*
1796	125.1	
		6.9
1806	243.8	
		3.0
1820	368.0	
		6.3
1830	677.4	
		7.5
1840	1396.4	

(Mitchell and Deane, 1962, pp. 131)

The census takes up the story in 1841, and we may then follow it (with a splice in 1881 and another in 1911) all the way to 1981. I pick out four industries or groups of industries, standard-bearers of the Industrial Revolution, to measure and illustrate what was going on. Their progress is shown in Table 5.5.

Until 1911, the census emphasised the occupations of the individuals whom it counted; in 1911, two sets of tables were presented, one grouped by occupations, the other by industries. From 1811 to 1831, the emphasis was on the number of families dependent on three groups of services, trades, crafts or industries for their living. Each of these viewpoints has its own peculiar appeal.

In Table 5.5 I take a somewhat different viewpoint, seeking the number of workers to whom each of the four industries give support. The precision with which it is possible to do this improves with the series 1911–81, in which a distinction is made between classification by industry and by occupation. Fortunately, the distinction before 1911 was not so important, for most of the workers in each industry were in fact process (production) workers, their occupations directly concerned with making the product.

But with the advance of technology, the number of process workers in an industry became less and less representative of the industry as a whole. In 1907, the Census of Production showed that in the 'production industries' (manufacturing, mining, construction, gas, electricity and water) white-collar employees constituted 7.0 per cent of the workforce. By 1948, the proportion had doubled. The advance of the white-collar brigade has continued, for example in manufacturing industry:

	Males	*Females*
	%	%-
1948	15.2	17.9
1984	28.2	29.1

(Department of Employment, *Historical Abstract 1886–1968*, pp. 408 and 276, and *Employment Gazette*, November 1984, p. S19.)

The proportion of maintenance craftsmen has also increased as machines have displaced production workers. Thus it is to the industry tables that we must turn to determine the number of workers to whom the production of a group of products gives employ.

In Table 5.5, the data from 1841 to 1881 are occupation-orientated. From 1881, second line, to 1911, first line, those engaged in trading in the products of the industry are included. From 1911, second line, traders are excluded, but white-collar, maintenance and other

Table 5.5   Employment in four industries, 1841–1981 (in thousands, indexes 1841 = 100)

	Textiles		Metal-making and using		Mining		Railways
	Nos	Index	Nos	Index	Nos	Index	Nos
1841	785	100	302	100	195	100	2
1851	1182	151	476	158	305	156	29
1861	1181	150	652	216	385	197	60
1871	1181	150	777	257	439	225	97
1881	1153	147	880	291	513	263	158
	1299	147	1026	291	612	263	234
1891	1352	153	1210	344	758	326	296
1901	1349	153	1569	445	937	403	444
1911	1464	166	1923	546	1210	520	603
	1359	166	1999	546	1128	520	
1921	1305	159	2564	700	1305	602	622
1931	1338	163	2466	673	1166	538	538
1941	871	106	3753	1025	820	378	—
1951	997	122	4025	1100	861	397	528
1961	790	96	4256	1163	722	333	462
1971	591	72	4220	1153	391	180	230
1981	288	35	3118	852	281	130	181

Sources: 1841–81, Booth, Table 1.1 above. 1881–1911, Mitchell and Deane (1962) p. 60, except Railways: census tables, inc. platelayers, gangers, packers, railway and railway contractors' labourers and navvies. 1911–81, census industry tables, except 1941: *British Labour Statistics Historical Abstract*, p. 218.

Table 5.6   Percentage of United Kingdom exports provided by textiles, metal-making and -using, coal and chemicals in various years, 1911–71

	1911	1925	1938	1951	1971
Textiles	29.3	29.2	15.2	18.1	4.8
Metal-making and -using	18.4	19.0	31.6	60.8	56.3
Coal	6.9	5.9	7.6	1.3	0.3
Chemicals	3.6	2.5	4.1	7.5	9.4

Sources: 1911–38, Mitchell and Deane (1962), pp. 283–4; 1951, *Annual Abstract of Statistics*, 1957, p. 222; 1971, *Annual Abstract of Statistics*, 1979, pp. 315–6.

ancillary workers are added. In the indexes these difficulties are avoided by chain-linking the series in 1881 and 1911 so that continuity is achieved.

For Britain, the nineteenth century was a period of textile-led growth. Employment in the metal-making and metal-using industries grew faster, but from so much smaller a base that it was only after 1891 that it caught up. Indeed, textiles continued to dominate British exports until 1928. Table 5.6 shows the percentage of the export earnings of the United Kingdom in various years between 1911 and 1971 provided by the major export industries.

Coal continued to play an important role until 1938. Metal-making and metal-using (which includes the manufacture of machines, electrical equipment, vehicles and ships) surpassed textiles in 1929; by 1938, their export sales were double those of textiles. Chemical exports rose steadily as textiles and coal fell.

For a period of three centuries, Britain's greatness depended on its textile industry, with wool dominating until the end of the eighteenth century and cotton from the beginning of the nineteenth. The shops that shaped the British mentality were drapers' shops, their products paying for foreign wars and conquests. The textile mills of the nineteenth century reshaped the British countryside; in them, British workers were drilled and dragooned into the world's first proletariat. A textile business in Manchester enabled Engels to follow the hounds, financed the writing of *Capital*, and paid for music and dancing lessons for the little Marx girls. Textiles paid, too, for the mean back-to-back houses of Yorkshire and Lancashire, and the great Victorian mansions of Belgravia.

In 1911, the United Kingdom supplied 57 per cent of world exports of cotton yarns and thread, and 59 per cent of cotton manufactures. In that year, Japan contributed 4 and 3 per cent and India 5 and 1½ per cent respectively (Committee on Industry and Trade, *Survey of Textile Industries*, HMSO, 1928, pp. 156–7).

Of course, the collection of industries represented in Tables 5.5 and 5.6 helped one another along, the activities of each complementing in various ways those of the others, and all dependent on the infrastructure in which industrial societies grow. Steam-engines were first used to pump water out of coal-mines and raise and lower their skips. Their application to railroads provided an immense new outlet for iron and steel, as did the mechanisation of factory production. The application of the Bessemer process to steel-making, by means of which the cost of steel was reduced from about £40 per ton in 1860 to £4 or £5 in 1895, had repercussions throughout the world of transport and production.

We have been considering two aspects of industrial growth: the number of workers supported by different industries and their contribution to foreign earnings. But production does not depend only on the size of the labour force, for output per worker was also growing as a result of advances in technique and improvements in organisation and experience. To incorporate this, we turn to indexes of industrial production that measure changes in output in terms of real product: tons of coal, pig iron or steel, or weighted indexes averaging the growth in a number of key products. A less direct method is to calculate sales in money terms and deflate (or inflate, as the case may be) by applying a price index.

Charles Feinstein (1976) has constructed production indexes for a number of industries for the years 1855 to 1948 or 1965. To continue the series, we may splice it to that produced since 1946 by the Central Statistical Office. Table 5.7 presents indexes of output for three industrial groups for census years between 1861 and 1981. To these we apply the indexes of employment from Table 5.5 to calculate indexes of output per worker. If output has gone from 100 to 120, while employment has gone from 100 to 110, output per worker will have moved from 100 to $120/111 \times 100 = 109.09$.

Tables 5.5 and 5.7 give us maps of employment and output of the most important British industries – the blueprint, as it were, of British industrial history. They all rose strongly to 1911, though the fluctuations of the trade cycle made the journey a rough one. The outbreak of war in 1914 forestalled an impending economic crisis. The collapse of 1921 was followed by the growth of the infant

Table 5.7   Indexes of output and output per worker in textiles, mining and quarrying, and metal-making and -using, 1861–1981

	Textiles		Mining and quarrying		Metal-making and -using	
	Output	Per worker	Output	Per worker	Output	Per worker
1861	100	100	100	100	100	100
1871	136	136	142	125	180	151
1881	145	148	182	136	257	190
1891	174	171	216	131	308	194
1901	166	163	251	122	429	208
1911	202	182	311	118	522	206
1921	132	125	190	62	508	157
1931	163	150	262	96	723	232
1951	236	291	256	127	2260	444
1961	219	342	228	135	3104	577
1971	284	592	193	212	3946	739
1981	183	796	145	220	3429	870

Sources: To 1931, Feinstein (1976), Table 52; except mining and quarrying, Table 51. From 1951, *Annual Abstracts of Statistics*. For metal-making and using, Feinstein's series have been combined using the following weights: 1861–1913, percentage employment in 1886 from Board of Trade (1893), ferrous metal, 8.9; shipbuilding, 17.8; engineering etc., 73.3. 1913–48, percentage employment in census 1921 industrial tables: ferrous metal, 10.04; ships, 15.88; mechanical engineering 52.61; electrical engineering 6.84; vehicles, 14.63. From 1948, weights as shown in *Annual Abstract*.

electrical and motor industries, and all forged ahead in the post-war boom of 1951. By 1971, employment had dipped but production in textiles and metals reached new heights. There followed a relapse, the end of which is not yet in sight.

Output per worker, however, has continued its upward path. A textile worker of 1981 produced (on average) as much as eight textile workers of 1861. Over the same period, output per miner more than doubled, and per metal-worker rose almost ninefold.

Of course, these statistics are descriptive rather than econometric. The use of different indicators of industrial production and of different weights would yield different answers, though it is to be hoped that the general impression would be confirmed.

5.5 THE PROFESSIONALS

There is deep aesthetic pleasure to be gained by watching crafts-people at work, the hands exercising a magical power as they transform 'natural goods into useful goods' (Loebl, 1976, p. 22). The uninitiated marvel at the order and beauty of the result.

Professionals are not required to exercise manual dexterity, nor physical strength and endurance, unless, like surgeons or pianists, they belong to that small group whose jobs combine cerebral power with delicacy and assurance of touch. Instead, they are the custodians of culture whose instrument is the mind. To perform their vocation they must learn, memorise and master a body of knowledge, and seek to extend its boundaries. Of course, there are some who do nothing of the sort: having obtained their qualification, they direct their efforts to extend not knowledge but their own wealth and prestige. Professional skill may be used to resist progress and promote illusion. So we must judge the quality of an age not only by the number of professionals it supports but by their creativity and the liveliness of their ideas. Thus qualified, this number, and its proportion in the economically active population, are a measure of economic and social progress.

We can get a view over 140 years by fitting together data drawn from Tables 1.1, 2.1, 3.1 and 4.2. The coverage in Table 5.8 is not entirely consistent, so that the series goes from 1841–81, 1881–1911 and 1911–81.

In 1841, in every 1000 of the gainfully occupied population, 25 were professionals; in 1981, the proportion had multiplied by nearly 6, to 147 per thousand. In the fourth column of Table 5.8, you see the percentage increase in the numbers of professionals from one census year to the next. The final column is a measure of how the *proportion* of professionals in the economically active population has advanced. Between 1921 and 1931 it reached its lowest rate of growth, only 2.2 per cent above that of the total labour force, but there then followed fifty years of growth that accelerated with the passage of time. Between 1971 and 1981, when the occupied population grew by 1.5 per cent, the number of professionals grew by 34.4 per cent. Their proportion of those occupied went from 11.1 per cent to 14.7 per cent – an increase of 32.4 per cent.

In the early decades, there were considerable increases between 1841 and 1851, and again between 1871 and 1881. We see from Booth's figures (Table 1.1, pp. 4 ff) that in each case it was medicine and education that led the pack and, again in each case, that the main increases were amongst the women:

		000s	
		1841–51	*1871–81*
Doctors, nurses and medical auxiliaries	M	+ 7.1	+ 5.8
	F	+12.1	+ 7.4
Teachers	M	+ 8.0	+16.4
	F	+38.1	+37.2.

Over the next thirty years, numbers increased by one-fifth in each decade. Between 1881 and 1911, there was an increase of 71 per cent. This time, nurses and others in the subordinate medical service led the field:

	1911 as % of 1881

Nurses, subordinate medical services	230
Literary and scientific pursuits	214
Clergymen, priests, nuns	172
Medical doctors	157
Engineers and surveyors	154
Teachers	150
Lawyers	129
Art, music, drama, exhibitions, games	124
All	171

We have covered the seventy years from 1841 to 1911 in two steps; the next seventy years I propose to cover in one. The census authorities have invented various mysteries to make this difficult (the fifty-year lapse in the production of consolidated tables for Great Britain, juggling with status categories, and the amalgamation of manual occupations across skill boundaries), but with much labour and occasional guesswork it remains possible. It is easiest with the professions, where occupations are clearly recognised, their scope and function vigorously defended by those who practise them. To make comparison easier, I return to the division, applied in Chapters 3 and 4, between higher and lower professions. The former are shown in Table 5.9.

There were 18 286 000 in the occupied population in 1911, and 25 406 000 (rounded to the nearest thousand) in 1981. So to maintain

Table 5.8 Numbers and proportions of professionals (higher and lower), 1841–1981

	Nos (000s)	% of occupied population	%growth in nos	proportions
1841	183	2.5	—	—
1851	276	2.9	50.9	16.0
1861	318	3.0	15.5	3.4
1871	372	3.1	16.7	3.3
1881	464 / 457	3.6 / 3.6	24.9	16.1
1891	551	3.8	20.6	5.5
1901	674	4.1	22.3	7.9
1911	796 / 744	4.3 / 4.1	18.1	4.9
1921	875	4.5	17.6	9.8
1931	968	4.6	10.6	2.2
1951	1493	6.6	24.2[a]	19.8[a]
1971	2770	11.1	36.3[a]	29.7[a]
1981	3724	14.7	34.4	32.4

[a]Rate per decade compounded.

Sources: Tables 1.1, 2.1, 3.1, 4.2 above.

Table 5.9 Numbers in the higher professions, 1911 and 1981

	1911 Men	1911 Women	1981 Men	1981 Women	All 1911	All 1981
Churchmen women	44610	7972	31950	4140	52582	36090
Lawyers	25598	1	45840	8080	25599	53930
Doctors (medical)	26086	611	61230	19440	26697	80670
Dentists	8747	322	14330	3460	9069	17790
Engineers	9858	16	359500	5950	9874	365450
Surveyors	4547	—	78140	1430	4547	79570
Scientists[a]	4692	170	90060	22890	4862	112950
Economists			7510	2770		10280
Social scientists	—	—	3870	3230	—	7100
Accountants	11378	29	92150	9460	11407	101610
Authors[b]	13031	1856	36800	18570	14887	55370
Architects, town planners	10561	19	35200	2730	10580	37930
Officers, armed services	14261	—	28650	1080	14261	29730
All	173369	10996	881370	100000	184365	981370

[a]inc. mathematicians.
[b]inc. editors and journalists.

Sources: Census occupational tables.

its proportionate size in the population, any occupation, between those years, would have had to grow by 40 per cent. All the higher professions have done better than that except the church, where clerics have fallen in number by more than 30 per cent. For every 10 000 of the occupied population there were 28 in 1911, and 14 in 1981. They did very well between 1841 and 1911, more than doubling in numbers; after that, the established churches languished, though Catholic priests, monks and nuns continued to increase. After 1951, the distinction disappeared. Between 1951 and 1981, there was a drop in numbers of 10 000.

The numbers in most professions rose by a factor of two or three in the seventy years, but all the rest were overshadowed by the proliferation of engineers and scientists:

	1981 as % of 1911
All higher professionals	532
Engineers	3701
Scientists	2323

Let us now add architects and surveyors to engineers and scientists and measure the growth in numbers of these professions by whose genius the natural world is controlled and adapted (wisely or otherwise) for the edification of the human race. The data are presented in Table 5.10.

Table 5.10   Engineers, scientists, architects, surveyors and ship designers, numbers and percentage changes, 1911–81

Census year	*Nos (000s)*	*As % of previous census year*
1911	30	—
1921	48	160
1931	71	148
1951	187	162[a]
1961	378	202
1971	502	133
1981	558	111

[a] Rate per decade compounded.

Sources: Bain (1966), p. 307, and census occupation tables.

We may see now how profound a change took place over the years of the First World War. This was the period of the technological revolution occasioned by the attempts of the great nations of Europe to kill one another. In 1911 in Great Britain there were fewer than 5000 scientists and fewer than 10 000 engineers. Over the previous thirty years they had been increasing by a few hundred per year; then, between 1911 and 1921 by 18|000. Between 1921 and 1931, a further 23 000 were added, and between 1931 and 1951, more than 100 000. The rate of increase reached its peak between 1951 and 1961 and then declined.

Surveys of the statistics reveal many false horizons – or answers that, on closer scrutiny, turn out to be questions. The facts act as constraints upon the imagination, which, without them, is free to think up the most satisfying hypotheses (or *theories*, as they are often mistakenly termed). Why the great leap between 1951 and 1961? By 1951, rationing had ended and post-war adjustments made; unemployment was well below half a million; the increase in output per person employed (at constant prices) rose by an average of a little more than 2 per cent per year. The market for British manufactures still seemed limitless, as did the need for housing and road construction. We were enjoying a post-war boom, itself maintained by the military adventures in progress in the Far East.

The censuses provide a few more data to help in the interpretation of Table 5.10. It was the mechanical engineers who scored the highest increase between 1951 and 1981. The electrical and electronic engineers came second, not first as I would have thought:

	1981 as % of 1951
Mechanical engineers	426
Electrical and electronic engineers	323
Surveyors	235
Architects, town planners	214
Civil, structural, municipal, mining	
Metallurgists	150
Chemical and gas	104

But in addition to these increases, there were 115 000 engineers distinguished in 1981 who were included somewhere in the above categories in 1951, the largest group being the 45 000 planning and quality control engineers who were not separately listed in the earlier year.

Our study of professional employment emphasises the contrast between Britain before and after the First World War. In the nineteenth century and until 1914, Britain was in a sub-industrial phase, dominated by the textile industry. For the ensuing sixty or seventy years, it was a fully industrial state. Some analysts have been led to designate the present phase as 'post-industrial society', a proposition from which a lively literature has emerged (ushered in by Daniel Bell, 1974).

The lower professions (as defined in the census social class divisions and applied here) encompass somewhat less than three times the numbers included in the higher professions. But whereas women comprise only 10 per cent of the higher professionals, they form nearly 57 per cent of the lower. Table 5.11 compares numbers in the main occupations in this class in 1911 and 1981.

Table 5.11 Numbers in the lower professions, 1911 and 1981

	1911		1981		All	
	Men	*Women*	*Men*	*Women*	*1911*	*1981*
Teachers	76680	202076	373810	464440	278756	838250
Nurses	1525	94291	78590	682410	95816	761000
Technicians	—	—	226740	47230	—	273970
Subordinate medical services	4554	3625	57800	57690	8179	115490
Draughtsmen	—	—	97160	9350	—	106510
Social welfare workers	—	—	61190	118030	—	179220
Artists[a]	8700	4518	41510	21580	13218	63090
Officers, pilots (ships and aircraft), air traffic controllers	14054	—	43130	840	14054	43970
Actors, entertainers	9523	9493	23090	12580	19016	35670
Photographers, cameramen, sound & vision operators	—	—	29770	5490	—	35260
Librarians	7624	4042	9060	18830	11666	27890
Pharmacists	9974	364	13540	7130	10338	20670
Musicians	24817	26284	14320	4810	51101	19130
Sportsmen	—	—	9400	4170	—	13570
Veterinary surgeons	2880	3	4330	1050	2883	5380
Literary, artistic and sports workers n.e.c.	—	—	4980	21010	—	25990
All the above	160331	344696	1088420	1476640	5055027	2565060

[a]Including designers and window dressers in 1981

Sources: Census occupational tables.

Nurses and teachers constituted 35 per cent of the class in 1911, and 58 per cent in 1981. Between these two years, the number of nurses multiplied by nearly eight, the teachers by three. Those in the subordinate medical service increased fourteenfold, though from a very much smaller base, and mainly by the proliferation of the specialist functions applied in medical testing and treatment. It is heartening to see the increase in the numbers of artists, actors and entertainers, and sad to notice the decline in the number of musicians.

Some occupations have come to prominence that were not regarded as sufficiently important to distinguish in 1911, amongst which are draughtsmen, laboratory, engineering, architectural and building technicians, social welfare workers, and photographers, cameramen and sound recorders.

The growth of the professions represents an immense enrichment of the labour force, and an immense extension of opportunities for interesting and rewarding jobs. In Table 3.1 it was noted that in 1911 the higher and lower professions constituted 4.05 per cent of the occupied population; in Table 4.2 that in 1981 their percentage had grown to 16.72. It also represents a diversification of opportunities for women, with their invasion of medicine, law, accounting, pharmacy and various branches of engineering. As their expectations rise, so will the strength of that invasion.

5.6 THE OFFICE WORKERS

Office work lacks much of the intellectual interest of the professions, yet it provides an escape from the arduousness of manual labour. It is also, as already noted, an index of industrial advancement. That is not to say that a growth in the numbers of clerks represents an improvement in the technique of production: to a certain extent it does, in so far as it is a reflection of higher planning and organisation; but for the rest, it signals the fact that while manual labour has been reduced by the development of machines, the technique of office work has lagged behind. I have suggested that the application of electronics to communication and bookkeeping may at last have reversed the trend. In section 5.8 below we shall see what the statistical evidence suggests.

Meanwhile, Table 5.12 takes the story up to 1981. Until 1921, the total number of clerical workers was galloping ahead even faster than

Table 5.12   Clerical workers, 1881–1981 (in thousands)[a]

	All		Males		Females	
	Nos	% of occupied population	Nos	% of occupied males	Nos	% of occupied females
1881	208	1.63	201	2.27	7	0.19
1891	284	1.96	262	2.62	22	0.49
1901	418	2.56	346	3.00	71	1.49
1911	547	2.99	401	3.10	146	2.7
	887	4.84	708	5.48	179	3.30
1921	1300	6.72	736	5.40	564	9.90
1931	1465	6.97	817	5.53	648	10.34
1951	2404	10.68	990	6.35	1414	20.40
1961	3066	13.32	1120	7.26	1945	25.67
1971	3749	13.90	1013	6.38	2466	26.99
1981	3761	14.80	887	5.71	2874	29.09

[a]1881–1911, first line: commercial or business clerks, excluding clerks in banks, insurance, law, railways and the public service. 1911, second line, to 1981, all clerks, as well as credit agents and collector salesmen.

Sources: Census occupational tables.

that of the professionals. Between 1931 and 1951, the rate of increase averaged 28 per cent per decade; between 1951 and 1961, almost the same – 27.5 per cent. But between 1961 and 1971 it fell to 22.3 per cent, and between 1971 and 1981 the total rose by only a fraction of one per cent.

The growth in the army of clerks is a striking feature of the development of the labour force. In 1911 one worker in twenty was a clerk; in 1981, one in seven. Real domestic product per head of occupied population has more than doubled in the same period, but the interaction between these two developments is complex. To some extent, the clerks have helped to create the additional wealth; to some extent the existence of the additional wealth has required additional clerks to look after it.

Another curious feature illustrated by Table 5.12 is the manner in which women, after their late start, in due course became numerically dominant in the clerical labour force. Out of 208 000 'commercial or business' clerks in 1881, only 7000 were women: that is, 0.19 per cent of gainfully occupied females. One hundred years later, clerical workers formed by far the most important group, with 29 per cent of all employed women. We get intimations of the surrounding circumstances from various commissions and committees of inquiry into the civil service, in particular the Playfair Commission appointed by Disraeli's government in 1874. At that time, written communications and letters had to be done by hand, and men copyists were employed at ten pence an hour to do it. But now they were being substituted by boy clerks at 4d an hour, a process facilitated by the 'vastly increasing means of education' that was enabling the middle class to 'fairly compete with, if not beat, the men in the upper class' (First Report of the Playfair Commission, 24 December 1874, para. 1919). In those days, people took class distinctions for granted and were quite willing to talk about them. In the 1980s, when in some respects they are just as strong, it is not done to mention them. Thus, according to Knox, Principal and Estimate Clerk of the War Office:

> If the junior establishment is to be a success, it must be taken from a class of life considerably inferior in social position to that from which the seniors are taken. The men in that class should be men who would be regarded more as inferiors, like the lower class of men employed as clerks in a solicitor's or in a merchant's office — men of a humbler position than the seniors — men whom you could put to do work of a merely mechanical kind, all of which is supervised. (Playfair Commission, para. 22).

And Bamford of the Accountant and Controller-General's office:

> If a man aspired to rise to a superior position I would make him prove his right to that position; for instance, if he dropped his 'h's' or had not the habits of a gentleman, even if he were clever in every other respect, he should remain on the lower establishment. I think that if we once admitted people of a naturally inferior order to the regular establishment, that indescribable sense of what is right and fitting which now exists in the service would perish. (para. 1273)

What chance did women have in these circumstances? They were admirably fitted for work as domestic servants, teachers (ministering to children), nurses (ministering to the sick), but the office remained a man's world. It is strange that they should have been employed so widely in the textile industry. Perhaps this was because spinning and weaving had until the nineteenth century been a cottage industry, and in any case was largely a phenomenon of the north. But evidence given to the Ridley Commission of 1886 indicates an important change of mood (this was a Royal Commission 'To inquire into the Civil establishments of the different offices of state at home and abroad'; it is their second report to which I shall refer).

This change in mood was promoted by the invention of the typewriter, which was found to be eminently suitable for operation by 'lady typewriters', and by the intransigence of the men writers or copyists who, as noted, were already being replaced by boy clerks at less than half their rate. Being temporary civil servants, the copyists were not constrained by an age bar. A senior clerk from the Civil Service Commission testified that they were drawn from amongst every class in society, 'from ex-military and naval officers down to mechanics', though the majority of them came from the lower part of the middle class, 'sons of small tradesmen and clerks and such people' (Playfair Commission, First Report, para. 22). Writers had at first been hired from a firm of law stationers who were paid 10d an hour, of which the men received 8d. Then in 1871, the task of hiring was allotted to the Civil Service Commission and the writers were given the full 10d. They soon formed a Writers' Association and began agitating to become established Civil Servants, with permanent tenure and rights of promotion, so that Lowe, who was Chancellor at the time, came to regret the decision:

> I think that we overlooked two or three things which we ought to have seen, or which are now at least very evident. One thing which we overlooked was the danger of collecting a very large body of persons together, having friends all over the country, having a particular interest, and that interest being to obtain better terms from the Government. I think that we overlooked the political aspect of the question. Certain gentlemen have found it very expedient to make political capital out of the alleged grievances of these writers; and I now think that it is a pity that there were collected together some three thousand persons, or something of the kind, for this sort of employment, all having a common interest to press upon the Government the raising of their wages. (Playfair Commission, First Report, para 3123)

In newspaper production, linotype eliminated hand-setting and, in our own day, has been eliminated by electronic word processors. So in the 1870s and 1880s the turbulent writers, with their beautifully crafted script, were eliminated by the typists.

Women were introduced into the Returned Letter Office of the

Post Office in 1873, and their employment was cautiously extended. Some of the Playfair commissioners were disturbed at the moral implications: 'Is there not that qualification, namely, that you are obliged to have all the letters examined in order to see that there is no indecent letter before you pass them to the women?' (para. 3874). By the end of 1874, there were 1308 women clerks employed in the telegraph department and 116 in the postal division of the Post Office. Members of the Commission were concerned that they might come into contact with members of the public or with male clerks, and that there would be a high labour turnover. The Receiver and Accountant-General was able to reassure them: separate rooms were arranged for men and for women. It was true that 'they go off with rapidity just now', but since it took only about six months for them to become efficient, the public got a cheap service – a very cheap service indeed, so that the average cost of a clerk in the Telegraph Service had been reduced from £103 12s 6d per year to £41 14s 9d. But would it be possible to continue the lower remuneration, seeing that the ladies gave the same quality of work as the men? 'Unfortunately', the Accountant-General replied, 'there is an abundant supply of poor gentlewomen with a sufficient amount of education for almost any work required by us; gentlewomen of limited means, daughters of officers in the army and navy, and of clergymen and medical men' (Playfair, para. 4569).

By the time of the Ridley Commission (1886), the employment of women had been accepted. Sir Algernon West recommended their use 'in all type-writing business': 'They are accurate, they are quick, they are cheap and there is no superannuation'. While the men copyists received 36s per week, 'the type-writers have 17s to 23s a week. Then they must come to us qualified. That is skilled labour. The superintendent has 25s to 30s'. There was no difficulty 'in carrying out proper arrangements for separation consistent with decorum' (Ridley Commission, Second Report, paras 19368 *et seq.*)

Thus fears were assuaged, costs reduced, and a great new field of employment opened to female endeavour.

5.7 PAY PATTERNS

In Table 5.2 we looked at some estimates of how average wage rates moved between 1801 and 1981, with the changes in the prices of the goods and services that wage earners spent them on. According to these indexes, wage rates rose 27 per cent between 1801 and 1811, fell between 1811 and 1841, then set off on an upward path, interrupted by declines in the decades of 1911 and 1931.

Prices fell 46 per cent between 1801 and 1851, rose until 1871, then in 1891 returned to much the same level as in 1851 and there rested until 1911. In 1911, real wage rates were about double their level of 1811. Even so, the question of how a civil service copyist could live on 36s a week daunts the mind. Bricklayers earned about the same, though they had to work much longer to do so: 56½ hours a week in London in the 1870s, compared with the copyists' 42. Bricklayers' labourers got only 23s 6d at that time. But, of course, in those days a farthing was quite an important coin. John Burnett (1969) collects data from nineteenth century household budgets in his chapter 4.

The Department of Employment presents statistical series on wage rates and hours of work for various manual occupations, going back to the early years of last century (*British Labour Statistics Historical Abstract*, 1971, pp. 28–38), but it is not until the last quarter of the century that there is available systematic data about white-collar earnings with which to compare it. Within the civil service, pay moved as shown in Table 5.13.

In general, the lower paid did better than the higher paid and the women did better than the men. The highest paid did worst of all, but not very much worse than the three much less highly paid classes who came next in the hierarchy. The professional engineers, however, did best of all, in keeping, perhaps, with the telephone service, whose growth coincided with the advent of the electrical age.

Between 1876 and 1913, money (or nominal) pay rates rose moderately and, because prices in 1913 were little different on average from those of 1876–9, the changes in money and real pay were almost identical. Between 1913 and 1978, by contrast, prices multiplied almost eighteen times and pay, on average, fifty-four, so that real earnings had almost tripled. In Table 5.14 I show the average pay in 1978 of men and women in various occupational classes and the factor by which it had multiplied since 1913.

As in the years 1876–1913, women have done better than men and the lowest paid have done better than the higher paid. The women's average has been pulled down by the fact that semi-skilled workers, of whom there are a great many, have done considerably worse than the men, while there are very few women managers and administrators, who have done very well and much better than the men. But despite this, on average women are three points ahead on current

Table 5.13   Civil service pay, 1876–1913

	Av. pay per year 1876–9 (£)	Pay in 1913 as % of av. for 1876–9
Permanent heads of departments	1920	101.6
Administrative class	530	103.4
Executive class	184	105.8
Clerical officers[a]	184	105.8
Clerical officers[b]	78	148.8
Women clerks	79	140.0
Postal and telegraph officers (males)[c]	84	123.4
Postmen and sorters	60	138.4
Postal and telegraph officers (females)[c]	51	151.1
Post officers engineers (professional)	264	177.9
Post office engineers (manual)	76	125.5

[a]In 1876–7, second and lower division clerks.
[b]In 1876–9, assistant clerks or abstractors, into which class the writers and copyists had been absorbed.
[c]Men or women telegraphists or counterclerks and telegraphists.
Source: Routh (1954), pp. 206 and 211.

Table 5.14   Average pay of men and women by occupational class, 1978, and factor of increase since 1913–14

	Pay per annum, 1978 (£)		Multiple of 1913–14	
	Men	Women	Men	Women
Higher professional	8286	6712	26	—
Lower professional	5435	3892	35	44
Managers and administrators	8050	5070	40	63
Clerks	3701	2730	37	61
Foremen, forewomen	4685	3214	38	56
Skilled manual	4354	2246	41	51
Semi-skilled manual	3827	2356	55	47
Unskilled manual	3390	2275	54	81
Averages, current weights	4786	2691	51	54
Averages, 1911 weights	4241	2516	45	50

These incomes match the occupational classes whose numbers are shown in Tables 3.1, 4.2 and 4.3 above.

Source: Routh (1980), Table 2.27, pp. 120–1.

weights and five points ahead on 1911 weights.

The difference between the averages on current weights and on base (1911) weights measures the rise in the averages caused by the migration of the employed from lower-paid to higher-paid classes. If there had been no such change, male income would have averaged £4241 in 1978, but because of upward migration it reached £4786, an increase of 12.8 per cent. For women, the upward shift has produced a rise of 7.0 per cent.

Women have managed to score some quite substantial relative increases: for lower professionals, their pay was 57 per cent of men's in 1913–14, and 72 per cent in 1978; for the clerks it went from 42 per cent to 74 per cent. But overall, on current weights, it has risen only three percentage points – from 53 per cent to 56 per cent.

Clearly, an important attribute of any profession is its 'worth' in terms of other professions: the relative value that society, in its own mysterious ways, attaches to it. Of course, we are not talking of moral worth, but of how much those who employ or engage them are prepared to pay. Nowadays, an increasing number of organisations try to work this out on some logically satisfying basis by using systems of job evaluation. The figures shown in Table 5.14 are the result of averaging the results of multitudes of such schemes. Using higher professionals as the standard of value, we may summerise the outcome in the terms shown in Table 5.15.

In systems of job evaluation, jobs are ranked in order of importance, with credit allocated for their need for education, training, knowledge, skill, experience, judgement, authority, dexterity, and so on, and compensation awarded for exertion, danger, dirt, boredom and other adverse attributes. In this way it is possible to establish a hierarchy of jobs and thus determine the rank that any specified job should enjoy. But it is not possible to say from this how much one rank should be paid relative to any other. For this, the work study experts resort to custom and practice: the generally accepted view of how much more a professional engineer should get than a fitter, a foreman than those he controls, a manager than those he manages, and so on. As the terms 'custom and practice' imply, these views are often accepted for lengthy periods, but they may be disturbed by brief periods of turbulence during which accepted views are overthrown. Periods of slow change are then interrupted by efforts at restitution by those who feel their status has been lowered, their privileges infringed. So it is possible to distinguish nine major periods in the pay history of Great Britain between 1914 and 1978,

Table 5.15   Equivalent of one male higher professional in other
                    occupations, 1913–14 and 1978

	One male higher professional equalled	
	In 1913–14	*In 1978*
Males		
Lower professionals	2.1	1.5
Managers and administrators	1.6	1.0
Clerks	3.3	2.2
Foremen	2.7	1.8
Skilled manual workers	3.1	1.9
Semi-skilled manual workers	4.75	2.2
Unskilled manual workers	5.2	2.4
Females		
Higher professionals	—	1.2
Lower professionals	3.7	2.1
Managers and administrators	4.1	1.6
Clerks	7.3	3.0
Forewomen	5.75	2.6
Skilled manual workers	7.5	3.7
Semi-skilled manual workers	6.6	3.5
Unskilled manual workers	11.7	3.6

Source: as for Table 5.14.

the net outcome of which is measured in Tables 5.14 and 5.15. These
periods are listed in Routh (1980), pp. 178–80.

There is one other important element against which these phenom-
ena must be viewed: though the pay structure within an organisation
may be logically and morally acceptable, *between* organisations no
such attributes apply. The result is a dispersion of earnings for any
specified occupation generally much wider than the differentials
between different occupations. You will see this in the tables of the
New Earnings Surveys showing median, quartiles and deciles of
earnings. Thus in any specified industry, many unskilled workers will
be earning more than many skilled workers, clerks than professionals, etc. There are no 'market rates' strong enough to
eliminate these differences.

5.8   DIRECTIONS AFTER 1981

Directions and pace of change after 1979 were influenced by the
combined weight of depression and monetarism, each reinforcing the
other. To measure the outcome we shall have to wait for the

publication of the occupation tables of the population census of 1991. However, we can get an indication of what is going on from the findings of the New Earnings Survey (NES). This, as the name suggests, is principally concerned with the measurement of earnings (by industry, occupation, age and sex). But in order to do this, it takes a random sample of about 1 per cent of employees in employment, and publishes the numbers in each occupation, though not, as a rule, if less than 100 men or women (as the case may be) in the sample were employed in it.

Let us see what we can discern of current trends by a comparison of the data for April in the years 1981 and 1985. There are a number of features that detract from the value of the NES material as extensions of that from the census. The NES includes only employees in employment. This leaves out the unemployed (a serious omission in 1981 and still more so in 1985), as well as employers and the self-employed. In the occupied population revealed by the census of 1981, 21.2 per cent of the males and 11.2 per cent of the females belonged to the categories excluded.

Of course, if this affected all occupations similarly, the class proportions revealed by the NES and the census would remain commensurate, but it does not. In the census tables for 1981, amongst the males, employees in employment accounted for only 14 per cent of farmers, horticulturists and farm managers, 47 per cent of the building and construction workers, 44 per cent of the lawyers, 53 per cent of doctors and dentists, and 71 per cent of architects and town planners.

Another disadvantage is the size of the sampling error. It is bad enough in the census, which since 1961 has been based on a 10 per cent sample. With the NES and its 1 per cent sample, it is more than three times greater, and for small occupations is quite serious. For instance, an occupation for whom the NES picked up 100 representatives would suggest a population of 10 000 in the labour force. But, at two standard errors, the odds are 20 to 1 that the number in the whole population would lie between 9400 and 10 600, an uncomfortably wide gap for comparisons between years.

Thus we cannot say how the occupational class numbers derived from the NES would compare with those from the census; we can, however, pick up something useful by measuring how the *proportions* between the classes compared at the beginning and the end of a specified period of years. These are shown, for 1981 and 1985, in Table 5.16.

Table 5.16   Percentage distribution of men and women between occupational classes in the New Earnings Survey, April, 1981 and 1985

| | | 1981 | | | 1985 | | |
		M	F	All	M	F	All
1A	Higher professions	7.0	0.8	5.0	7.4	0.9	5.1
1B	Lower professions	10.3	21.2	13.9	10.4	23.6	15.0
2B	Managers, etc.	18.0	5.8	14.0	17.7	6.7	13.8
3	Clerks	7.6	44.2	19.7	9.0	44.1	21.4
4	Foremen/women, etc.	6.4	1.9	4.9	5.2	1.3	3.9
5	Skilled manual	23.6	2.5	16.6	23.2	2.2	15.8
6	Semi-skilled manual	21.9	20.3	21.4	21.8	18.2	20.5
7	Unskilled manual	5.2	3.3	4.5	5.3	3.0	4.5
		100	100	100	100	100	100

For method of calculation, see text.

Sources: Department of Employment, *New Earnings Surveys, Part D, Analysis by Occupation.*

As anticipated, the fit between the census and the NES is not good (see Table 5.17). For the men, the NES overstates Classes 1 to 4 and understates 5, 6 and 7. For women, the NES greatly overstates the lower professions and the clerks, is quite near for managers, and understates everyone else. In each case, in Table 5.17 I am comparing the percentage distribution between occupational classes of employees in employment in April 1981.

Note that in Table 5.16 the absolute numbers of those in the occupational classes are not commensurable because the sample was 6¼ per cent smaller in 1985 than in 1981. Only those in occupations

Table 5.17   Percentage distribution between occupational classes, April 1981

| | | Males | | Females | |
		Census	NES	Census	NES
1A	Higher professions	5.9	7.0	0.9	0.8
1B	Lower professions	8.6	10.3	16.6	21.2
2B	Managers and administrators	16.2	18.0	5.3	5.8
3	Clerks	6.8	7.6	31.3	44.2
4	Foremen/women etc.	6.2	6.4	2.8	1.9
5	Skilled manual	26.0	23.6	5.3	2.5
6	Semi-skilled manual	23.3	21.9	28.9	20.3
7	Unskilled manual	7.0	5.2	8.9	3.3
		100	100	100	100

identifiable as belonging to one of the eight occupational classes have been included. Thus we lose the residuals included in the headings but not allocated to specific occupations in the NES. This arises from the Department of Employment's unwillingness to list separately occupations covering less than 100 employees.

Despite all these difficulties, we can reach some conclusions. The first is that we are looking at a rather sick society, with the forces that have been so conspicuously at work in former years now sadly muted. They are, however, working in the same general direction, with Classes 1 to 3 still expanding while the others contract (though the proportion of unskilled manual workers has remained stationary).

It is disconcerting to see the decline, relatively and absolutely, in the number of engineers: the total number of men embraced in the survey in 1985 was 93 per cent of that of 1981, but the total of engineers in the latter year was only 89.2 per cent of the former. The only bit of comfort in this respect was the growth in electrical and electronic engineers by a quite respectable 5.5 per cent. The number of nurses, too, rose substantially, both male and female: by 21.7 per cent for the men and 12.5 per cent for the women.

I had been anticipating the much-heralded decline in the number and proportion of clerical workers as the electronic revolution took effect. You may remember that the number of males did decline between 1961 and 1971, and still more substantially between 1971 and 1981, though the total in the group continued to rise (Table 5.12 above). Now in Table 5.16 we see the strange phenomenon of a rise in the number of men, while the proportion of female clerks among all female employees declines fractionally. Perhaps, as in the case of nurses, men are turning to clerical work for want of other employment?

Our attempt to uncover current trends has revealed a state of stagnation. Somewhere, the new technology is no doubt struggling to get out, but it will have to wait awhile before it succeeds and demonstrates in what direction it is going to take us.

6 Britain in its World Setting

6.1 PARTNERS AND COMPETITORS

We have compared Great Britain with itself at various points of time, and witnessed the great enrichment of job options open to its inhabitants. The descendants of the agricultural labourers, mill workers and domestic servants of the last century have advanced and diversified into jobs that spare the muscles and exercise the mind. Of course, as I write, over three million would-be workers have no jobs at all, and are condemned to a life of boredom and frustration, while a majority of the rest still have jobs that use little of their intellectual potential. None the less, generation by generation advances have been and are being made, with sons and daughters entering fields beyond the reach of their parents. To conclude our investigation we should examine data from some other countries against which Britain's achievements may be assessed. I refer to 'partners and competitors', for the world is today much more of an economic entity than in earlier times. The establishments of the multinationals support one another across national boundaries, while their subsidiaries abroad may compete with their rivals at home. Scientists, technicians and managers move to and fro about the world to extend their training. Ideas and techniques cross and re-cross national frontiers.

At the end of the nineteenth century, Britain's industrial supremacy seemed secure. Henry Gibbins found that the United Kingdom accounted for between one-fifth and one-quarter of world trade: 'No other nation has as yet come within half this remarkable percentage. The three nearest competitors are Germany with nearly eleven per cent, France with about nine per cent, and the United States with over nine per cent' (Gibbins, 1903, pp. 487–8). But the technology of that time was still on a somewhat elementary level compared with what lay ahead and, in the 1920s, Britain floundered while other countries advanced.

Of course, British exports and imports no longer dominate world trade, but that has ceased to be a criterion of economic power except in the singular case of Japan. Instead, Table 6.1 uses as indicators of

Table 6.1   Occupied population by occupational group in various countries in the early 1980s

	Year	Total (000s)	0/1 Prof. (%)	2 Managers (%)	3 Clerks (%)	6 Farm, etc(%)	7/8/9 Production (%)
Israel	1984	1359	22.8	5.2	17.8	4.8	28.4
Canada	1984	11000	16.4	10.7	17.1	3.4	28.5
USA	1984	105005	15.7	11.0	15.9	3.4	28.5
Sweden	1984	4255	28.2	2.4	12.3	5.1	29.6
Denmark	1984	2720	19.4	2.4	16.2	2.3	29.3
Britain	**1981**	**25406**	**14.7**	**5.7**	**17.1**	**2.4**	**24.9**
Australia	1984	6462	15.7	6.8	18.1	6.9	33.4
Netherlands	1981	5548	18.0	2.4	17.2	5.0	27.0
Norway	1984	1970	20.9	6.4	10.8	7.0	31.3
German, FR	1984	26608	15.0	3.8	18.8	7.0	31.3
Italy	1981	22350	11.6	16.2	9.7	9.4	20.9
Japan	1984	57660	9.2	3.7	17.7	8.7	36.7
Hungary	1980	5069	14.7	0.7	12.1	10.0	50.6
Spain	1984	10274	8.5	1.6	11.2	5.4	34.5
Ireland	1983	1309	14.2	2.3	14.1	14.9	30.2
Bulgaria	1982	4479	17.3	2.2	8.0	19.7	41.7
Poland	1978	17962	11.0	1.5	13.9	26.7	37.4
Portugal	1984	4095	7.4	1.3	12.4	23.5	32.6
Yugoslavia	1981	9359	9.9	1.6	9.5	26.9	31.5
Greece	1983	3808	9.3	1.6	8.4	27.6	28.0
Egypt	1982	10115	11.2	2.0	8.6	38.3	24.4

For notes, see text.

Sources: ILO, *Year Book of Labour Statistics 1985*, Tables 2B or 2C, except Poland and Bulgaria, *Year Book 1982*, and Hungary, *Year Book 1983*. Great Britain, *Census 1981, Economic Activity, GB*, Table 3.

the quality of the labour force the proportion engaged in professional, managerial or clerical occupations and, inversely, the proportion engaged in agriculture. The emphasis is on professional training, literacy, numeracy, interest, and intellectual rather than physical effort. I ignore the not unimportant questions of end-product and wealth: the fact that many white-collar workers are employed in dubious financial pursuits or on the design and production of instruments of destruction, and that real income varies considerably between countries.

The *Year Book of Labour Statistics* offers a convenient source of comparative data. The statistics are standardised by the governments who supply them in accordance with the rules of the *International*

Standard Classification of Occupations (ISCO) (Geneva: ILO, revised edn 1968) and the *International Standard Classification of all Economic Activities* (New York: United Nations, revised edn 1968). The choice of countries is narrowed by the fact that many have not sent in data for occupational distribution, at least in recent years. This applies to some important Latin American countries as well as to the USSR, China, India, France and the United Kingdom. None the less, Table 6.1 includes the major capitalist industrial countries and some from Eastern Europe, with a few still in the early stages of industrial development.

Fortunately it is possible to adapt the categories of the 1981 census for Great Britain to conform with those laid down in ISCO, and this I have done. Note, though, that the ISCO major groups differ in some respects from the occupational classes used in Chapters 3, 4 and 5 above, so that the proportions shown for Great Britain in Table 6.1 are not identical with those of Tables 4.2 and 4.3.

ISCO Major Group 0/1, Professional, Technical and Related Workers, presents no difficulties, but Major Group 2, Administrative and Managerial Workers, curiously excludes farmers and farm managers as well as managers and working proprietors in wholesale and retail trade, hotels, restaurants and other catering and lodging services. It also excludes post- and station-masters.

Major Group 3, Clerical and Related Workers, is, by contrast, wider in scope than Occupational Class 3. It includes workers not immediately recognisable as clerks: postmen, bus and train conductors, storekeepers and telephone and telegraph operators. It also includes 'transport and communications supervisors' whom I have put among the foremen and supervisors in Occupational Class 4.

Major Group 6 includes farmers and farm managers as well as employees, employers and the self-employed in agriculture, forestry, fishing and hunting. Major Group 7/8/9 also fails to discriminate between skilled, semi-skilled and unskilled work. It includes occupations 'associated primarily with the extraction of minerals, the processing of materials and the fabrication and repair of products, including buildings ... operating transport equipment ... and non-agricultural labouring occupations' (ISCO, p. 17). To simplify matters, I have omitted sales workers (Group 4) and service workers (Group 5) as well as Major Group X (workers not classified by occupation) and the armed forces. You will, of course, find them included in Tables 2B and 2C of the *Year Books of Labour Statistics*.

Countries in Table 6.1 are ranked according to a formula consisting of the sum of the percentages engaged in Groups 0/1, 2 and 3, minus the percentage in Group 6. The first three groups are positively related to the level of industrial development, the percentage engaged in agriculture inversely so. (This does not mean the amount of agricultural *output*, for Canada and the USA, with by far the largest agricultural output, have a very small proportion engaged in producing it.) I have not included Group 7/8/9 in the ranking process because of its propensity first to grow and then decline with economic development.

6.2   THE BRITISH POSITION

Despite its marked progress in the 1950s and 1960s, Britain has lagged behind in professional growth. In Sweden nearly three workers in ten are in the professions. Nine other countries are in advance of Britain in this respect, while Hungary is its equal.

The proportion of managers and administrators is more difficult to interpret: why does Italy need so many, how can Hungary get on with so few? Britain had 5.7 managers per hundred compared with 10 or 11 for Canada and the United States. But Sweden, Denmark and the Netherlands all had only 2.4, Bulgaria 2.2 and Ireland 2.3. Perhaps there is an inverse correlation between managers and clerks, so that the Germans get on with 3.8 managers per cent because work has been delegated to the 18.8 per cent of clerks? It will take some enterprising research student with a taste (and the funds) for travel to answer these questions.

Table 6.1 does not distinguish between the sexes, but the data may be seen in Tables 2B and 2C of the *Year Book*. One measure of the advance of women consists of the proportion of women among the professional group. In Denmark, they constitute 62.5 per cent of professional workers; in Canada, Israel, Norway, Sweden and Portugal between 52 and 55 per cent, in the United States 48.4 per cent, in Australia, Ireland and Italy just over 46 per cent. In Britain, the proportion is 44.4 per cent, less than Japan (45.5 per cent) but more than Germany (41.0 per cent), Spain (38.5 per cent) and Egypt (28 per cent).

Britain's undistinguished record is, of course, worsened by the run-down of its education system that has been a feature of recent years. It is perhaps reassuring that this is a result not of inexorable economic forces but of purposefully designed, and therefore reversible, government policy.

Appendix: Allocation of 1981 Occupational Units to Occupational Classes

Class 1A: Higher professional
Unit
001   Judges, barristers, advocates, solicitors
002 1 Chartered and certified accountants
    2 Cost and works accountants
004 1 Economists, statisticians, actuaries
012 3 Social and behavioural scientists
014   Clergy, ministers of religion
015 1 Medical practitioners
    2 Dental practitioners
019   Authors, writers, journalists
024   Scientists, physicists, mathematicians
025   Civil, structural, municipal, mining and quarrying engineers
026   Mechanical and aeronautical engineers
027   Electrical and electronic engineers
028   Engineers and technologists n.e.c.
031 1 Architects and town planners
    2 Quantity surveyors
    3 Building, land and mining surveyors
041   Officers, UK armed forces
042   Officers, foreign and Commonwealth armed forces

Class 1B: Lower professional
004 2 Systems analysts, computer programmers
009 2 Officials of trade associations, trade unions, professional bodies and charities
    4 Librarians and information officers
    5 Legal service and related occupations
    8 Professional workers and related supporting management and administration
010   Teachers in higher education
011   Teachers n.e.c.
012 1 Vocational and industrial trainers
013   Welfare workers
016   Nurse administrators, nurses
017   Pharmacists, radiographers, therapists n.e.c.
020 1 Artists, commercial artists
    2 Industrial designers (not clothing)

	3	Clothing designers
	4	Window dressers
021		Actors, musicians, entertainers, stage managers
022		Photographers, cameramen, sound and vision equipment operators
023	1	Professional sportsmen, sports officials
	2	Literary, artistic and sports workers n.e.c.
029		Draughtsmen
030		Laboratory and engineering technicians
032		Officers (ships and aircraft), air traffic planners and controllers
033		Architectural and town planning technicians, building and civil engineering technicians, technical and related workers n.e.c.
068	2	Nursery nurses
070		Ambulancemen, hospital orderlies
138	1	Laboratory assistants

Class 2A: Employers and proprietors
All employers *except* those in Occupational Classes 1A and 1B.
Those self-employed in the following categories:

038	Wholesale and retail distribution
039	Hotels, clubs, etc., and entertainment and sport
040	Farmers, horticulturalists

Class 2B: Managers and administrators
All managers *except* those in Occupational Classes 1A and 1B. Including 'other employees' and 'self-employed without employees' in the following categories:

002	2	Cost and works accountants
	3	Estimators
	4	Valuers, claims assessors
	5	Financial managers
	6	Underwriters, brokers, investment analysts
	7	Taxation experts
003		Personnel and industrial relations managers; O & M, work study and operational research officers
005		Marketing, sales, advertising, public relations and purchasing managers
006		Statutory and other inspectors
008		Local government officers (administrative and executive functions)
009	1	Company secretaries
	3	Property and estate managers
	6	Management consultants
	7	Managers' personal assistants
012	2	Education officers, school inspectors
037		Office managers
044		All other managers
057	1	Importers, exporters, commodity brokers
	5	Sales representatives
	6	Sales representatives (property and services), other agents

Class 3: Clerical workers
All in Census Class 6, clerical and related, *except* those self-employed with employees, and excluding 051, 052 and 053, and including in addition:
035   Clerks of works
057 4 Credit agents, collector salesmen *except* self-employed with employees and managers

Class 4: Foremen, supervisors, inspectors
All foremen and supervisors *except* those in Occupational Classes 1A and 1B, self-employed with employees or clerical workers, but including:
137 1 Inspectors, viewers (metal, electrical goods)
138   Inspectors, viewers, examiners (*not* 138 1 Laboratory assistants)

Class 5: Skilled manual workers
051 3 Radio and telegraph operators
061   Policemen (below sergeant), firemen, prison officers
064   Chefs, cooks
074   Hairdressers, barbers
075 4 Undertakers, *except* managers
    5 Bookmakers, *except* managers
079   Agricultural machinery drivers and operators
085   Tannery and leather workers
087   Textile workers
091   Bakers, flour confectioners
092   Butchers
094   Paper board and paper product makers, bookbinders
096   Glass and ceramics furnacemen and workers
097 1 Rubber process workers, moulding machine operators, tyre builders
098 8 Wood and paper process workers
100   Printing workers, screen and block printers
102 1 Tailors, tailoresses, dressmakers
    2 Clothing cutters, milliners, furriers
103   Coach trimmers, upholsterers, mattress makers
105 1 Carpenters and joiners
    2 Cabinet makers
    4 Pattern makers (moulds)
106   Sawyers, veneer cutters, woodworking machinists
107 2 Dental technicians
    4 Musical instrument makers, piano tuners
    5 Glass and ceramics
    7 Leather
   10 Rubber
109   Furnacemen (metal), rollermen, smiths, forgemen
110   Metal drawers, moulders, die casters, electroplaters, annealers
112 1 Press and machine tool setters
    2 Centre lathe turners
    3 Machine tool setter-operators
113 2 Metal polishers
115   Tool-makers, tool fitters, markers-out

116   Instrument and watch- and clock-makers and repairers
117   Metal-working production fitters and fitter/machinists
118   Motor vehicle and aircraft mechanics
119   Office machinery mechanics
121   Production fitters, electricians, electricity power plant operators, switchboard attendants
122   Telephone fitters, cable jointers, linesmen
123   Radio, television and other electronic maintenance fitters and mechanics
125   Plumbers, heating and ventilating fitters, gas fitters
126   Sheet-metal workers, platers, shipwirghts, riveters, etc.
127 1 Steel erectors, benders, fixers
128   Welders
130   Goldsmiths, silversmiths, engravers, etchers
131 1 Coach and vehicle body builders
    3 Metal-making and treating workers n.e.c.
    6 Electronics wiremen
    7 Coil winders
       Trainee craftsmen (engineering and allied trades)
133 1 Pottery decorators
    2 Coach painters
    4 Painters and decorators n.e.c., french polishers
135 2 Instrument assemblers
140   Building and construction workers *except* 5 Handymen, general building workers
145   Face-trained coalmining workers
150   Rail transport operating staff
155 1 Mechanical plant drivers, operators (earth-moving and civil engineering)
    2 Crane drivers, operators
157 1 Warehousemen: 36.8 per cent of numbers shown for storekeepers, warehousemen, males; 7.8 per cent, females
161 2 All others in miscellaneous occupations n.e.c.

Class 6: Semi-skilled manual workers
051 2 Telephone operators
053 1 Postmen, mail sorters
055   Shop salesmen and assistants, shelf-fillers, petrol pump, forecourt attendants
056   Roundsmen, van salesmen
058   NCOs and other ranks, UK armed forces
059   NCOs and other ranks, foreign and Commonwealth forces
062   Other security and protective service workers (inc. traffic wardens)
065   Waiters and bar staff
066 1 Counter hands, assistants
068 1 Domestic housekeepers
    3 Other domestic and school helpers
069 1 Travel stewards and attendants
072   Caretakers

075 3   Launderers, dry cleaners, pressers
075 6   Service workers n.e.c.
077   Farm workers
078   Horticultural workers, gardeners, groundsmen
080   Forestry workers
082   Fishermen
083   All other in farming and related
089   Chemical, gas and petroleum process plant operators
097 2   Calendar and extruding machine operators, moulders (plastics)
098   All other in processing materials (other than metal) *except* 8 Wood
        and paper
102 3   Sewers, embroiderers
105 3   Case and box makers
107 1   Labourers and mates to woodworking craftsmen
    3   Carpet fitters
Others making and repairing:
    6   Wood
    8   Clothing and related
    9   Paper goods and printing
  11   Plastics
  12   All other (excluding metal and electrical) n.e.c.
112 4   Machine tool operators
113 1   Press, stamping and automatic machine operators
    3   Fettlers, dressers
127 2   Scaffolders, stagers
131 2   Galvanizers, tin platers, dip platers
    4   Oilers, greasers, lubricators
    5   Riggers
    8   Shot blasters
    9   Other metal, jewellery, electrical production workers
133 3   Other spray painters
135 1   Assemblers (electrical, electronic)
    3   Assemblers (vehicles and other metal goods)
137 2   Packers, bottlers, canners, fillers
140 5   Handymen, general building workers
141 1   Railway lengthmen
    2   Road surfacers, concreters
    4   Paviors, kerb layers
142 2   Mains and service layers, pipe jointers
143 1   Civil engineering, craftsmen's mates
146 1   Miners (not coal), quarrymen, well drillers
    2   Construction workers n.e.c.
148   Deck, engine-room hands, bargemen, lightermen, boatmen
152   Bus, coach, lorry drivers, etc.
153 1   Bus conductors
155 3   Fork-lift, mechanical truck drivers
157 1   Storekeepers: 52.3 per cent of numbers shown for storekeepers,
       males; 13.4 per cent, females
158 1   Slingers

    2   Workers in transport operating, materials moving and storing and related n.e.c.

160 7   Coal-miners, general labourers

Class 7: Unskilled manual workers

053   Messengers

057 2   Market and street traders and assistants

    3   Scrap dealers, general dealers, rag and bone merchants

066 2   Kitchen porters, hands

069 2   Hospital porters

    3   Hotel porters

072 2   Cleaners, window cleaners, chimney sweeps, road sweepers

075 1   Railway stationmen

    2   Lift and car park attendants

141 3   Roadmen

142 1   Sewage plant attendants

143 2   Building and civil engineering labourers

153 2   Drivers' mates

157 1   Warehouse and storemen's assistants: 10.8 per cent of numbers shown for storekeepers, warehousemen, males; 78.8 per cent, females

    2   Stevedores, dockers

    3   Goods porters

    4   Refuse collectors, dustmen

160   General labourers, except 7, coal-miners

161 1   Boiler operators

17   Inadequately described and not stated.

Bibliography

ARMENGAUD, ANDRÉ (1970) *Population in Europe 1700–1914* (London and Glasgow: Fontana).

BAIN, GEORGE SAYERS (1966) 'The Growth of White-Collar Unionism in Great Britain', *British Journal of Industrial Relations*, vol. 10, no. 3.

—— and PRICE, R. (1972) 'Union Growth and Employment Trends in the United Kingdom', *British Journal of Industrial Relations*, vol. 10, no. 3.

BELL, DANIEL (1974) *The Coming of Post Industrial Society* (London: Heinemann).

BENJAMIN, BERNARD (1970) *The Population Census* (London: Heinemann).

BEVERIDGE, WILLIAM (1960) *Full Employment in a Free Society* (London: Allen & Unwin).

BOARD OF TRADE (1893) *General Report on the Wages of the Manual Labour Classes in the United Kingdom* (London: Eyre and Spottiswoode).

BOISGUILLEBERT, PIERRE LE PESANT (1843) *Dissertation sur la Nature des Richesses* (first published c. 1707; reprinted Eugène Daire, ed, Paris: Chez Guillaumin Libraire).

BOWLEY, A. L. (1937) *Wages and Income since 1960* (Cambridge: Cambridge University Press).

BURNETT, JOHN (1969) *The History of the Cost of Living* (Harmondsworth: Penguin).

CHILDREN'S EMPLOYMENT COMMISSION (1842) *First Report of the Commissioners, Mines* (Shannon: Irish University Press series of British Parliamentary Papers, 1968).

COLE, G. D. H. and FILSON, A. W. (1951) *British Working Class Movements, Select Documents 1789–1875* (London: Macmillan).

COMMITTEE ON INDUSTRY AND TRADE (1926) *Survey of Industrial Relations* (London: HMSO).

COUNCIL ON ENVIRONMENTAL QUALITY (1982) The Global 2000 Report to the President (Harmondsworth: Penguin Books).

DEANE, PHYLLIS and COLE, W. A. (1969) *British Eonomic Growth 1688–1959* (Cambridge: Cambridge University Press).

DEPARTMENT OF EMPLOYMENT (1972) *Classification of Occupations and Directory of Occupational Titles*, 3 vols (London: HMSO).

—— (1971) *British Labour Statistics Historical Abstract 1886–1968* (London: HMSO).

FEINSTEIN, C. H. (1976) *Statistical Tables of National Income, Expenditure and Output of the UK 1855–1965* (Cambridge: Cambridge University Press).

GIBBINS, HENRY DE B. (1903) *Economic and Industrial Progress of the Century* (London and Edinburgh: Chambers).

HAMMOND, J. L. and HAMMOND, BARBARA (1949) *The Town Labourer, 1760–1932* (London: Guild Books).

JAMESON, LEANDER STARR (1897) *Cecil Rhodes: a Biography and*

Appreciation (London: Macmillan).

KNIGHT, ROSE (1967) 'Changes in the Occupational Structure of the Working Population', *Journal of the Royal Statistical Society*, Series A, vol. 130, no. 3.

LAWTON, RICHARD (ed.) (1978) *The Census and Social Structure, An Interpretative Guide to Nineteenth Century Censuses for England and Wales* (London: Frank Cass).

LENIN, V. I. (1978) *Imperialism, the Highest Stage of Capitalism* (first published 1916) (Moscow: Progress Publishers).

LOEBL, EUGEN (1976) *Humanomics* (New York: Random House).

LONDON AND CAMBRIDGE ECONOMIC SERVICE (*n.d.*) *The British Economy, Key Statistics 1900–1964* (London: Times Publishing Co.).

MALTHUS, THOMAS ROBERT (1798) *An Essay on the Principle of Population* (revised edn 1803).

MARSH, DAVID C. (1965) *The Changing Social Structure of England and Wales 1871–1961* (London: Routledge & Kegan Paul).

MITCHELL, B. R. and DEANE, PHYLLIS (1962) *Abstract of British Historical Statistics* (Cambridge: Cambridge University Press).

OFFICE OF POPULATION CENSUSES AND SURVEYS (1977) *Guide to the Census Reports Great Britain 1801–1966* (London: HMSO).

ROUTH, GUY (1954) 'Civil Service Pay, 1875 to 1950', *Economica*, vol. 21 no. 83.

—— (1965) *Occupation and Pay in Great Britain 1906–60* (Cambridge: Cambridge University Press).

—— (1980) *Occupation and Pay in Great Britain 1906–79* (London: Macmillan).

SMITH, ADAM (1776) *The Wealth of Nations* (reprinted Oxford: Clarendon Press, 1976).

WEBB, BEATRICE (1926) *My Apprenticeship* (reprinted Harmondsworth: Penguin, 1971).

WOOD, G. H. (1899) 'The Course of Average Wages between 1790 and 1860', *Economic Journal*, no. 36, vol. ix.

Index

For references to industries, occupations and occupational classes, see the List of Tables and Figures, pp. vii and viii.